CW00449258

PLATO

CRITO

Also available in BCP Greek Texts series:

PLATO
CRITO

Edited with Introduction,
Commentary and Vocabulary by
CHRIS EMLYN-JONES

Bristol Classical Press

Cover illustration: Plato, from a herm of the second century AD, probably based on a lost statue by Silanion carved during Plato's lifetime, ca 365 BC; Ny Carlsberg Glyptotek, Copenhagen.

Published in 1999 by
Bristol Classical Press
an imprint of
Gerald Duckworth & Co. Ltd
61 Frith Street
London W1D 3JL
e-mail: inquiries@duckworth-publishers.co.uk
Website: www.ducknet.co.uk

Reprinted 1999, 2001

© 1999 by Chris Emlyn-Jones

All rights reserved. No part of this publication
may be reproduced, stored in a retrieval system, or
transmitted, in any form or by any means, electronic,
mechanical, photocopying, recording or otherwise,
without the prior permission of the publisher.

A catalogue record for this book is available
from the British Library

ISBN 1-85399-469-3

Contents

Preface

This edition of Plato's *Crito,* with the first full commentary in English since John Burnet (1924), aims to provide a guide to the dialogue for readers of Greek who, while requiring detailed help with the language, also wish to have the opportunity to appreciate the subtleties of Plato's philosophical argument and literary form. A critical exploration of the main issues of interpretation raised by this dialogue, with some account of the extensive modern bibliography, has been attempted in the Introduction.

I wish to express my thanks to Marga Emlyn-Jones, Howard Jones, James Neville, William Preddy and Rosemary Wright for many valuable suggestions for the improvement of the Introduction and Commentary. I am also indebted to Chris Davey for technical assistance.

Chris Emlyn-Jones
The Open University
November 1998

viii

Notes on this edition

1. The text and indented section summaries reproduced in this edition are those of J. Adam, reprinted by Bristol Classical Press (1988). In order to make the new Introduction and Commentary usable also with other texts of *Crito* a double system of reference has been adopted throughout: Adam's section and line nos., e.g. III.18, are followed by the corresponding Stephanus reference in brackets, e.g. (44d1-2). The latter follows the lineation of the new edition of the Oxford Classical Text (OCT²: see abbreviations, below), which frequently differs slightly from that of the first edition (OCT¹).

2. Adam included no *apparatus criticus* in the text and this has not been added; however the frequent occasions when his text needs to be queried or raises problems of interpretation are discussed in the Commentary as they arise.

3. References to editions/translations of *Crito* and secondary literature by name and where appropriate page reference, relate to the Bibliography.

4. Abbreviations of the names of Ancient authors and their works follow the style of LSJ (9th ed.: see below). In addition the following abbreviations will be found in the Commentary:
DK (B1 etc.): Diels, H., and Kranz, W., *Die Fragmente der Vorsokratiker,* 3 vols, 6th ed. (Berlin, 1951-2).
GP Denniston, R.D., *The Greek Particles,* 2nd. ed., (Oxford, 1950).
LSJ Liddell, H.G., Scott, R., Jones, H.S., *A Greek English Lexicon,* 9th ed. (with Supplement) (Oxford, 1968)
OCT¹ Burnet, J., *Platonis Opera* I (Oxford Classical Text) (Oxford, 1900).
OCT² Duke, E.A., et. al., *Platonis Opera* I (Oxford Classical Text, new ed. containing *Crito,* ed. W.S.M. Nicholl) (Oxford, 1995).

5. There is no attempt at consistency in the transliteration of Greek names. The Latinised adaptation will be used for names commonly known in this form, e.g. Crito, Socrates; for less well-known names the Greek form will be retained. For convenience of reference in the Commentary, Socrates and Crito will be abbreviated as S. and C.

6. In using the Vocabulary, readers should note that, following Adam's Greek orthography in the text, some words normally found under *sigma* (e.g. συνδοκέω) will be listed under *xi* (e.g. ξυνδοκέω).

7. Section titles such as 'Prologue', 'Exhortation' etc. are all editorial, and, like the section divisions themselves, included merely to assist comprehension of the text.

Introduction

1. SETTING AND CONTEXT

Plato's *Crito* is a dramatic dialogue between two speakers, Socrates and his friend Crito. The year is 399 BC and the scene is the state prison at Athens very early in the morning two days before Socrates' execution. About a month has passed since Socrates' trial and condemnation to death on a charge of ἀσέβεια (impiety) — 'not acknowledging the gods which the city acknowledges, but introducing different new divinities. And he is guilty of corrupting the young'. This was the ἀντωμοσία (affidavit) submitted by the prosecutor, which survived up to the second century AD in the Metroon, the building in the Athenian Agora where public archives were kept, according to the orator and philosopher Favorinus, quoted by Diogenes Laertius, II. 40; a paraphrase of this indictment is also quoted by Plato on several occasions, e.g. *Ap.* 24b8-c1. Execution of sentence awaits the return of a sacred mission to Delos which left Athens the day before the trial and has not yet arrived, but will do so shortly; during the ship's absence the city must remain pure and no executions may take place (details in *Phd.* 58a-c, Xen. *Mem.* IV.8.2, and also n. on *Cri.* I.35-6 (43c9-d1)).

The dialogue represents Crito's last-ditch attempt to save Socrates' life by persuading him to escape from prison and seek refuge elsewhere in Greece. In reply Socrates refuses to contemplate such a move, explaining why escape would not be in accordance with justice (τὸ δίκαιον). In its dramatic presentation of a decisive moment from Socrates' last days *Crito* is traditionally associated with three other Platonic dialogues: *Euthyphro*, a conversation outside the King's Stoa in the Athenian Agora where Socrates is about to face a preliminary hearing of the charges against him, *Apology*, Socrates' defence speech, and *Phaedo*, Socrates' last meeting with his friends, before his death by drinking hemlock.

These four dialogues dramatise significant episodes within a sequence of events which, taken together, are designed to demonstrate the outstanding intellectual and moral qualities of Plato's teacher and friend, and in particular his steadfastness in the face of death. It is not known how, or even if these dialogues were connected in Plato's lifetime; their close association as a compositional group was made by Thrasyllus, the 1st century AD philosopher and astrologer to the emperor Tiberius. Thrasyllus divided up the whole of the Platonic corpus into tetralogies, by analogy with the sets of four plays (tetralogies) produced by Athenian tragedians in the Classical Greek theatre; the *Euthyphro-Apology-Crito-Phaedo* tetralogy was the first (D.L. III.56-8; for an attempt to relate the four dialogues as a kind of dramatic tetralogy, see Adam, xii). The artistic brilliance and strong dramatic cohesion of the group has given it almost canonical status through the ages as a reliable account which was composed, it is assumed, soon after the events. Yet, despite a number of intertextual links (see e.g. nn. on *Cri.* V.20-1 and 21-2 (45e3 and e4)) there is no evidence that these dialogues were composed together; indeed, the first three are usually assigned, on grounds of style and subject-matter, to the earliest period of Platonic composition (before c.385 BC), while the subject-matter of *Phaedo*, with its exposition of the Platonic Theory of Ideas, has usually been thought, on a developmental view of Plato's early thought, to indicate a considerably later period of composition (Vlastos (2), 45-80; on the compositional date of *Crito*, see further below, section 4 (iii) and n.22).

Socrates is famous for having written nothing himself.[1] The gap was filled not only, as we have seen, by Plato, but also by other friends and associates of Socrates who composed philosophical dialogues and memoirs, the so-called Σωκρατικοὶ λόγοι (Aristotle, *Poetics,* 1447b11) which, like the dialogues of Plato, presented versions of Socrates' life and beliefs (Clay, 23-47). Non-Platonic versions of the last days, though badly preserved compared with Plato's, differ from his account in significant respects, in particular over the content of Socrates' defence speech, or whether he even made one (Xen. *Apology*, 1ff.; Maximus of Tyre, III.1-8; see Ferguson, 209).

The hiatus between Socrates' sentence and execution caused by the sacred mission to Delos would have left his friends plenty of time for prison visiting (Plato, *Phd.* 59d1ff), and *Crito* was not the only literary re-creation of a conversation possibly held during such a visit. Diogenes Laertius (II.60, III.36) repeats a story that Crito's role as persuader of Socrates was originally filled by Aeschines of Sphettos (a prominent Socratic of whose work some short extracts survive: see Saunders, 377-9), but that Plato assigned the role to Crito out of emnity to Aeschines. Doubt over Diogenes' reliability by no means excludes the possibility that Aeschines did try to persuade Socrates to escape and that he may have even written a dialogue on the subject (for details see Burnet, 173).

---

[1]In *Phaedo* (60c-d) Socrates is said to have lately taken up composing verses in prison: adaptation of some of Aesop's fables and a *Prelude* to Apollo; nothing further is known about these.

A recently published literary papyrus, written in 4th century BC Attic Greek (Gronewald, 33), contains fragmentary remains of a conversation between Socrates and an unknown associate where Socrates defends himself against the reproach that he had failed to make a satisfactory defence at his trial, by asking whether, after living a reasonable life, he should be grieved at the approach of death: there is, moreover, no reason to suppose that death gives more pain or pleasure than life. This may satisfy Socrates, comes the reply from an unnamed friend, but what would he say to those who don't necessarily accept that pleasure and pain are the defining criteria? There, unfortunately, the text ends. The author of this fragment is unknown (Gronewald, 51-3, conjectures Aristippus of Cyrene, exact dates unknown, but roughly contemporary with Plato), but acceptance of approaching death (Socrates was 70 years old in 399) as a reason for Socrates' failure to make, as his friends saw it, a serious defence, or even as a reason for not wishing to escape from prison, is found elsewhere, notably in Xenophon: ἔπειτα τῶν ἑταίρων ἐκκλέψαι βουλομένων αὐτὸν οὐκ ἐφείπετο, ἀλλὰ καὶ ἐπισκῶψαι ἐδόκει, ἐρόμενος εἴ που εἰδεῖέν τι χωρίον ἔξω τῆς Ἀττικῆς ἔνθα οὐ προσβατὸν θανάτῳ. ('Then, when his friends wished to snatch him away, he would not comply, but instead appeared to be making fun of them, asking them if they knew of any spot outside Attica which was inaccessible to death.' (Ap. 23)). Xenophon was not actually in Greece during this period, but his later accounts undoubtedly draw on earlier versions of the story, or perhaps oral traditions, which differ in important respects from those of Plato, especially, as we shall see, in Socrates' arguments for choosing death rather than exile.

   Plato's Crito, then, must be viewed, like the other dialogues of the tetralogy, not as a definitive account of an incident from the last days of Socrates — about which, in a strict historical sense, we know very little — but as a version of events which exists in a complex contextual relationship with other accounts which are in some respects at variance with it. Of course, Crito is for us not just 'a version'; the almost total eclipse of other 'prison conversations' doubtless owes much to the greatly superior philosophical and literary qualities of Plato's creation, which have heavily influenced the judgement of subsequent generations, including our own. Yet in concentrating on the many and varied qualities of Plato's literary genius it will be important for us not entirely to forget the context from which it came.

2. THE DRAMATIC STRUCTURE
(i) Characters
There are only two characters in the Dialogue, Crito and Socrates. Crito was about the same age as Socrates and from the same Athenian *deme* of

Alopeke (*Ap.* 33d9). He was one of a group of friends, including Plato himself, who were prepared to stand surety for the fine which Socrates finally, and unsuccessfully, proposed as a penalty at his trial (*Ap.* 38b6). Crito also appears to have made an offer (not accepted) to pledge a sum of money to the court that Socrates would not escape before execution, with the intention of sparing him the indignity of prison (*Phd.* 115d7). He was a wealthy man who had at some time suffered from the attentions of συκοφάνται (sycophants) (*Euthd.* 304c3, Xen. *Mem.* II.9., and see n. on *Cri.* IV.4 (44e3)).

Crito was said (D.L. II.121) to have written seventeen dialogues, about which we know nothing beyond their titles. In Plato, besides his role in *Crito*, he features as the main respondent of Socrates in *Euthydemus*, where he is anxious to pick Socrates' brains about the value of sophists for the education of his son Kritoboulos. Not a great intellectual, he nevertheless has a great affection for Socrates, which is reciprocated: he is presented by Plato in *Phaedo* as the follower chosen by Socrates to minister to him during his last moments, and it is to Crito that Plato's Socrates utters his memorable last words: 'Crito, we owe a cock to Asklepios; see to it, and don't forget' (*Phd.* 118a7-8).

Crito's emotional reaction to Socrates' situation in *Crito* is sympathetically, even humorously portrayed, and his overwrought and occasionally confused syntax in the Prologue and Exhortation (Sections I-V) provides the perfect foil for Socrates' cool and reasoned response. Crito's positive contribution to the dialogue is confined to these initial sections where he represents an all too human regard for public opinion which he fears will censure him and Socrates' other friends for allowing the prisoner to die (see Commentary, summary of Section V). Through the rising tide of his exasperation with Socrates we catch glimpses of a wider background of friends and associates who are willing to help with money and influence (IV.20 (45b2)ff.), but who cannot comprehend why Socrates has failed to defend himself in an acceptable manner. Crito regards the whole episode of the trial as a disaster which could have been avoided, he believes, if Socrates had behaved properly, rather than letting down those who supported him (V.16-26 (45d9-46a3)).

After this convincing characterisation Crito then abruptly fades, dramatically speaking, into the background. The reduction of initially eloquent speakers to 'yes men' is a common feature of Plato's Socratic dialogues (cf. *Euthyphro, Gorgias*), but in *Crito* the transition of Crito into a monosyllabic supporter of the development of a case he has just argued elaborately against (VI.38 (47a6)ff.) seems particularly to lack dramatic plausibility. It may be that in *Crito* coherence of character has to come second to the overriding urgency with which Plato needs to make Socrates' case. It has also been suggested that Plato may be using Crito's intellectual

5

shortcomings to present a more subtle interaction between the two characters (see further below, section 4 (iii)).

The presentation of the character of Plato's Socrates, on the other hand, is consistent and harmonises with the other 'last days' dialogues in demonstrating his contempt for public opinion and his calm concentration, even *in extremis*, on the overriding importance of acting on the basis of correct ethical conclusions reached by mutually acceptable arguments (VI.1 (46b1)ff., IX.22-30 (48d9-49a2)); on the Platonic-Socratic ethics of the dialogue, see below, 3 (ii)).

Yet one feature characteristic of Plato's Socrates, ironic humour, is rather less evident in *Crito* than in other early Platonic dialogues, and the development of a full dramatic presentation of Socrates is abruptly terminated half-way through by the surrender of his *persona* to the Laws of Athens (XI.11 (50a8) ff.).

(ii) Dramatic form

At twelve Stephanus pages, *Crito* is the shortest of Plato's dialogues and employs the simplest of dramatic structures:[2] direct dialogue between two characters speaking tête à tête (*Ion* and *Euthyphro* also have this structure). The initial form follows in some respects a typical Platonic-Socratic pattern of a 'definition dialogue': a lightly but vividly sketched dramatic setting, an initial contribution by Socrates' respondent, followed by Socrates' questioning of the respondent in order to expose logical inconsistencies in his position. Following this questioning, however, *Crito* parts company with this pattern; instead of pursuing the argument further and concluding with an admission of failure, the reaching of an impasse (ἀπορία) with regard to whichever moral value is being argued about (cf. *Euthyphro, Laches, Lysis*), Socrates takes a very different tack and introduces an extended monologue by the Laws of Athens whose strongly expressed arguments against escape, couched in markedly rhetorical form, round off the dialogue.

Even where *Crito* does follow a typically Platonic-Socratic pattern, the content is very different. Crito's initial contribution (Sections III-V) is persuasive in intent rather than exploratory, and the balancing protreptic of the Laws at the end (Sections XI-XVI) underlines *Crito's* uniqueness; in other dialogues practical issues usually serve as a background for and introduction to theoretical discussion, whereas in *Crito* the position is reversed — Socratic philosophical arguments are used to underpin exhortation as to what practical steps should subsequently be taken. The discussion about definition, insofar as there is one, concerns justice (τὸ δίκαιον), but remains implicit; Socrates' chief purpose is to apply an

---

[2]If one excludes *Apology*, a group of three speeches usually included among the dialogues for convenience of classification.

uncontested application of τὸ δίκαιον — that it is unjust to do wrong even in retaliation for injustice (X.17 (49b7)ff.) — to the immediate question of what action is δίκαιον in this particular instance. Accordingly, in the middle part of the dialogue (Sections VI-X) Socrates runs unopposed through a number of ethical arguments — unopposed, because he presents himself as merely requesting assent for ethical positions on which he and Crito have long been agreed (ὡς πολλάκις ἡμῖν καὶ ἐν τῷ ἔμπροσθεν χρόνῳ ὡμολογήθη; X.4-5 (49a6-7)). This somewhat perfunctory exposition (with the dramatic development of Crito's character as the casualty (see above (i)) nevertheless has the important purpose of emphasising Socrates' consistency: the trial has done nothing to change his beliefs; what he earlier considered just still holds good (VI.8 (46b6)ff.).

The final argument section of the dialogue Socrates surrenders to 'the Laws'. He abandons his familiar questioning stance in order to conduct in the name of the Laws of Athens an extended series of arguments with himself (for discussion of these arguments, see below, section 3 (iii)). The sustained and forcefully rhetorical nature of this personification makes it unique in the dialogues (for details see n. on XI.10 (50a7-8)). The dramatic device of representing arguments as coming from outside himself allows Socrates to exhibit a certainty and authority which extend well beyond the quizzical stance he is accustomed to adopt. For the duration of this personification Socrates in propria persona adopts the role in which he normally places others; for once he becomes the compliant 'feed' (for another example from Plato, cf. Socrates' reported conversation with Diotima in Smp. 201dff.).

The effect of this device is underlined by Socrates' brief return to his own persona at the very end, when he says to Crito that he seems to hear the words of the Laws '...just as the Korybantes seem to hear the pipes, and this noise of these words booms in my head and makes me unable to hear any others' (XVII.2-6 (54d3-5)). This religious dimension, already present in Socrates' prophetic dream at the beginning of the dialogue (II.9-17 (44a6-b3)), appears elsewhere as a valedictory theme (Ap. 40c4ff., Phd. 107c1ff.). In Crito, even though in formal terms merely a simile, the reference to exotic religious rites, with extension of the musical image in αὕτη ἡ ἠχὴ... βομβεῖ ('this sound...hums [in my ears]'), seems to suggest a Socrates who has abandoned the hypothetical framework of the Laws' discourse as introduced at XI.8-11 (50a6-8) (εἰ...ἔροιντο 'if [the Laws] were to ask us...'), in order now to receive their advice as emanating from an unanswerable higher authority.

3. THE ARGUMENTS

The structure of arguments in Crito is tripartite: (i) the case Crito attempts to make in favour of Socrates' escape (III-V (44b6-46a9)) is followed by

(ii) Socrates' establishment of some fundamental ethical principles (VI-XI.7 (46b1-50a5)), leading to (iii) the third and final section, the arguments of the Laws (XI.8-XVI.19 (50a6-54d2)).

Philosophical interest in *Crito* has usually been focussed on the final section of the dialogue, the arguments of the Laws, around the nature and problems of which a vast bibliography has accumulated, whereas Crito's position has not usually attracted so much attention. Yet as a Socratic dialogue *Crito* runs true to form in the organic development of themes from one section to another: the earlier arguments foreshadow issues which are explored fully later on.

(i) Crito's Exhortation (III-V (44b6-46a9))

Having briefly mentioned the effect on him of the loss of an irreplaceable friend (III.4-6 (44b8-9)) Crito quickly pushes on to what emerges as his overriding concern: the effect that Socrates' execution would have on his own standing and that of Socrates' other friends in the eyes of the Athenian community, and the need, therefore, to react to popular, albeit ignorant, opinion: most people will believe erroneously that it was he, and not Socrates, who vetoed the escape through his unwillingness to part with the necessary bribes, and so sullied his own reputation: καί τοι τίς ἂν αἰσχίων εἴη ταύτης δόξα ἢ δοκεῖν χρήματα περὶ πλείονος ποιεῖσθαι ἢ φίλους; ('And yet what reputation could be more shameful than that of seeming to value money above friends?' III.9-10 (44c2-3)). The implication is that Socrates should be concerned, if not for his own, then surely for his friends' honour.

Concern about popular reaction also fuels the next argument, that Socrates ought not to be concerned about the practical consequences for his friends — loss of money and goods through attacks by συκοφάνται — since his friends are surely just (που δίκαιοι: IV.9 (45a1)) in being willing to run that risk, or worse, in saving Socrates — the force of which claim is rather spoilt by the addition that, in any case, the expenditure would not be great, and there are several associates also willing to pay: IV.14-23 (45a6-b6). His non-Athenian friends can also guarantee him a welcome abroad.

Crito's arguments are implicitly grounded in a concern for personal prestige which becomes explicit in the final part of the Exhortation. Just as it was δίκαιον for Crito and his friends to risk their livelihood on Socrates' behalf (IV.9-11 (45a1-3)), it is, in Crito's estimation, not δίκαιον for Socrates to betray himself (σαυτὸν προδοῦναι) and bring on himself the destruction which his enemies (ἐχθροί) intend (V.1-6 (c6-9)). Crito's conception of justice is based on a popular ideal of Athenian male excellence (ἀρετή), 'to help his friends and injure his enemies, while taking care to come to no harm himself' (*Meno* 71e). By this standard Crito judges himself and his friends as aspiring to live up to the ideal, and

Socrates as woefully deficient in failing to protect himself, his friends and his family from their enemies.

This conception of ἀρετή cuts across, and largely operates outside, the formal legal framework in which Socrates' supposed dilemma is set, since, for Crito, τὸ δίκαιον sets a value on what the Athenian citizen male ought to do as an individual in order to protect his personal interests and those of his friends and family (φίλοι) against his enemies (ἐχθροί). Accordingly any reference to the possible legal injustice of Socrates' sentence is strikingly absent from Crito's Exhortation, since such a consideration would be secondary to the purely personal need to defend Socrates against the 'enemies' who condemned him (see eg. Adkins, 231).

This leaves an unasked question, however: if defiance of the court's decision is δίκαιον for both Socrates and Crito, and compliance with the law the reverse (IV.9 (45a1),V.1(c6)), what attention should be paid to legal authority? The central dilemma of the dialogue is implicitly foreshadowed.

(ii) Socrates' reply

Socrates meets head-on Crito's concern for 'popular opinion' (ἡ τῶν πολλῶν δόξα, eg. III.18 (44d2)), first, by dismissing its *power* to change his mind by means of coercion or fear: the only way of convincing him is by deploying new and better arguments: VI.1-26 (46b1-d7).[3] His current predicament is merely an incidental happening (τύχη: VI.10 (46b8)), which does not of itself change his established view on essential questions of right and wrong.

Secondly, he questions the *value* of popular opinion by means of the argument from expertise: one should value the opinions of the wise, and these are those of the expert in a particular field, eg. physical training, where health will come from obeying the instructions of the knowledgeable instructor who possesses the requisite skill (τῷ ἐπιστάτῃ καὶ ἐπαΐοντι: VII.13-14 (47b10-11)), rather than that of the majority of people.

This principle of expertise, says Socrates, applies to other areas as well, especially to those currently under debate, eg. matters of doing what is just and unjust etc. which are related not to the body but, more vitally, to that part of us which is affected by just and unjust conduct (VII.25-VIII.18 (47c8-48a4)).[4]

---

[3]Socrates has already interjected into Crito's Exhortation a comment concerning the powerlessness of the many to do harm or confer benefit, through failure to know what they really want; but Crito does not allow Socrates to develop support for this position in this dialogue (for the developed argument, see esp. *Grg.* 466bff.).

[4]In *Crito* Plato presents Socrates as appearing not to know, or being unwilling to state here precisely. what part of the person. 'whatever it may be' (ὅ τί ποτ' ἐστὶ VIII.14

9

Socrates is here rehearsing two related lines of argument which are frequently found in Plato's dialogues: the primacy of conclusions reached by correct argument over force of numbers or influence (e.g. *Grg.* 472aff.) and the power of the expert as the person who has knowledge (e.g. *Ap.* 24c-25c, *Euthphr.* 4eff., *Grg.* 471e-72b). This latter argument makes use of the 'craft analogy', a bridge (as it appears to us) between craft knowledge and values: just as there are experts in, say, physical training so also there are experts in questions involving justice, injustice and the like. The rehearsal is here as brief as possible (Plato's Socrates elsewhere often produces more than one skill 'analogy', e.g. shoemaking, carpentry, medicine), and Crito's monosyllabic agreement ensures that progress is swift.

Having demolished the power and authority of popular opinion, Socrates next goes on to the question of what he ought to do. Socrates agrees with Crito to this extent — that what he should do must be δίκαιον, because this is the basis of 'living well' (τὸ εὖ ζῆν). Nevertheless he rejects as irrelevant (IX.4-19 (48c1-d6)) the popular associations of these terms which Crito has assembled in his previous argument: responsibilities to dependants and friends, consequences for one's own physical well-being etc. Accepting the value-term, Socrates proceeds to give it very different content.[5]

Socrates' argument, to all the stages of which Crito agrees, can be set out as follows:-

(1a) In no circumstances must one act unjustly (Οὐδαμῶς ἄρα δεῖ ἀδικεῖν): X.17 (49b7).

(1b) One must not, even when treated unjustly, return injustice, since in no circumstances must one act unjustly: (Οὐδὲ ἀδικούμενον ἄρα ἀνταδικεῖν...ἐπειδή γε οὐδαμῶς δεῖ ἀδικεῖν) (19-20 (49b9-10).

(1c) One must not do wrong (Οὐ δεῖ κακουργεῖν) — phrased as a question at 22 (49c2).[6]

(47e9)) corresponding to the body, is affected by knowledge (or ignorance) of justice and injustice. Elsewhere Plato's Socrates introduces this part, casually and apparently uncontroversially, as the soul (ψυχή); cf. *Grg.* 477a, *La.* 185e1-2. Socrates' reticence here may signify adaptation to Crito's essentially unphilosophical nature (see eg. Weiss, 43 n.12), or perhaps the need, dramatically, to move quickly through the argument.

[5]In Plato, as well as in popular thought, δικαιοσύνη and δίκαιος can be translated narrowly 'justice' and 'just', as distinguished from other 'cardinal virtues', eg. temperance, bravery, holiness; however, frequently the polarity δίκαιος/ἄδικος has a broader ethical range, = 'right/wrong' (as on most occasions in *Crito*).

[6]Translating κακουργεῖν thus rather than eg. 'inflict injuries' (Tarrant), in that the latter can imply merely physical hurt, which Socrates would in certain circumstances, eg. physically defending oneself in a battle, or inflicting just punishment, not regard as wrong, (see Kraut, 26n.2).

(1d) It is not just, having suffered wrong, to return it (οὐ δίκαιον κακῶς πάσχοντα ἀντικακουργεῖν) — also a question at 24-5 (49c4-5).

(1e) Doing wrong to people...does not differ from acting unjustly (Τὸ γάρ...κακῶς ποιεῖν ἀνθρώπους τοῦ ἀδικεῖν οὐδὲν διαφέρει): 27-8 (49c7-8). As elsewhere in *Crito*, Socrates states briefly positions underpinned more extensively in other dialogues (e.g. *Grg.* 474bff.), with which detail Crito is presumed (albeit improbably in the dramatic context[7]) to be familiar; cf. X.4-11 (49a6-b1).

(1a) is a proposition the formal terms of which Crito can emphatically endorse (X.18 (49b8)), since he has already implied as much in his Exhortation; but he is not yet apparently aware of (or does not recall?) the Socratic implications. Proposition (1b), which follows logically from (1a), finds Crito slightly less sure ('it seems not': Οὐ φαίνεται, 21 (c1)), but he agrees nevertheless. This and his further agreements to (1c)-(1e), especially (1d), will shortly be claimed by Socrates to undermine fundamentally Crito's case for the justice of avoiding execution. The weight these propositions will bear in the development of the subsequent argument is signalled by the elaborate care taken by Socrates (X.30-45 (49c10-e3)) to ensure that at this point Crito understands the argument and is sincere in his agreement.

The final two assertions, set in the form of questions, which Socrates makes in his own *persona* set the scene for the central arguments of the Laws which follow. They are:-

(2a) Should a person do those things which he has agreed with someone, if they are just, or should he practice deception? (πότερον ἃ ἄν τις ὁμολογήσῃ τῳ δίκαια ὄντα ποιητέον ἢ ἐξαπατητέον;): X.49-50 (49e6-7).

Crito accepts that the agreed things should be done; Socrates then proceeds to a question, the answer to which occupies the remainder of the dialogue:

(2b) In escaping from here without persuading the city [to let us go] are we or are we not doing wrong, and doing it to those to whom we least ought [to do wrong]? And are we, or are we not abiding by what we agreed to be just? (XI.1-5 (49e9-50a3)).

Crito confesses that he is not clear about (2b), presumably because the conversation has taken a characteristic Socratic path: having agreed to a progressive series of propositions one by one, Crito is then asked to make a choice the implications of which contradict his original contention —

---

[7]Crito is portrayed by Plato as someone who, though having been continually exposed to Socrates' teaching, does not appear to have absorbed it at all.

that it is just for Socrates to try to escape. The result for Crito is typical Socratic ἀπορία (impasse) (XI.6-7 (50a4-5)).

Yet a looming contradiction with his earlier assertions might not be Crito's only reason for puzzlement. The choices Socrates offers may also be difficult to make because the terms in which they are offered are (at this stage, deliberately) vague. In (2a) it is by no means clear what 'agreement' involves: whether δίκαια ὄντα refers to the content of the agreement or the terms under which it is made, or both (see e.g. Kraut, 32). This vagueness extends into (2b): the answer to this question would depend on what the agreement with the city is thought to involve, and without this clarification Crito simply cannot say whether or not Socrates' escape will constitute inflicting wrong on the city.

(iii) The arguments of the Laws of Athens

1. The Laws' case.

A. The initial incomprehension of associates is often used by Plato as a dramatic device for an expanded explanation by Socrates of a new or controversial idea (cf. *La.* 185b8). Here his expansion of (2a) and (2b) constitutes the essence of Socrates' case against escape. He makes the hypothetical assumption that Crito's arguments have persuaded him, and that they are both being confronted by 'the Laws and the community of Athens' (οἱ νόμοι καὶ τὸ κοινὸν τῆς πόλεως) and asked to justify their proposed course of action.

The Laws' arguments are not set out formally like those of Socrates in (ii) above, but the first group can be rendered in essence thus (see e.g. Bostock, 2ff. for a more formal analysis):-

(3a) A city cannot continue in existence and not be overturned, in which legal judgements reached by the courts (αἱ γενόμεναι δίκαι) have no force but are rendered invalid and destroyed by private individuals (XI.14-17 (50b2-5)).

(3b) By contemplating disobedience to this law (i.e. that implied in (3a), that legal judgements are binding) Socrates is intending, so far as in him lies, to destroy the laws and the whole city (σύμπασαν τὴν πόλιν) (12-14 (50b1-2); see also 20-1 (b7-8)).

The Laws regard (3b) as following logically from (3a), i.e. they appear to be associating defiance of one law — that 'judgements pronounced shall be binding' (τὰς δίκας τὰς δικασθείσας...κυρίας εἶναι: 20-1 (b8) — with destruction of law in general. The Laws are thereby clarifying (2a) above: 'things which [a person] has agreed' include, indeed seem principally concerned with, judicial verdicts. But, according to (2a), there is a proviso that such agreements need to be just (δίκαια ὄντα: X.49 (49e6)). This gives Socrates a possible answer to the Laws: the agreement with the Laws is not δίκαιον because the city was guilty (ἠδίκει...ἡ πόλις:

XI.22 (50c1)) of reaching a false verdict at his trial (22-3 (c1-2)). Crito evidently considers this an effective answer to the Laws (24 (c3)).

In strict logic, this could nevertheless be the end of the argument for Crito. He has already agreed to (1a) and (1b) (above section 3 (ii)) which forbid the return of injustice for injustice. So, *if* disobeying a legal verdict constitutes an injustice against the city (quite a big *if*: see below, 2), then Socrates must submit to the sentence of the court whatever the moral status of the original verdict in his case. Yet the Laws go on to try to substantiate this assumption at some length, obviously realising that the weakness of the argument lies in the assumption that disobedience is always an injustice, especially in a case where the disobedience happens to be a reaction to an unjust verdict.

B. This attempt takes the form of developing an elaborate analogy in which the Laws relate themselves to individual citizens as parent to child, or master to slave (XII.8-51 (50c10-51c3)). They have presided over the life of Socrates as Athenian citizen: the marriage of his parents which led to his birth, his upbringing and education. He is therefore the Laws' offspring and slave (καὶ ἔκγονος καὶ δοῦλος: 21 (50e3-4)), which means that his rights are not equal with theirs: just as children or slaves may not retaliate against a father or a master, so, to an even greater extent, citizens may not oppose their country. Socrates must either persuade it otherwise, or do and suffer whatever it requires of him. Anything else constitutes violence against the Laws.

While this may appear to dispose of the idea of justified disobedience for the moment, the Laws' analogy does not address the question of 'agreement', and indeed might be thought to count against it; operating the analogy for ourselves: do children or slaves have agreements with parents or masters? Compulsion over individuals with lesser rights, rather than the idea of agreement, seems to be uppermost in this passage (23-35 (50e5-51a7)).

C. In the next section, however, the Laws do attempt to graft the idea of 'agreement' onto the decidedly authoritarian 'parent/child' analogy. The Athenian state allows a citizen, once he has attained the age where he undergoes a *dokimasia* (scrutiny on 'coming of age' — see further n. on XIII.9 (51d3)), and if the city's laws do not satisfy him, to leave the city and go elsewhere without forfeiting his property. In these circumstances, however, remaining in the city is equivalent to a tacit agreement either to persuade the city otherwise or practise obedience to whatever it tells him to do (XIII.16-20 (51e2-5)). In this respect Socrates, having hardly ever travelled outside the city, may be assumed to be uniquely satisfied with the city's institutions, and so particularly obliged to comply with its verdicts

13

(XIV.5 (52a6)ff.). Having entered into the agreement without compulsion, deceit or time-pressure (39-40 (e1-2)), Socrates has chosen to remain in Athens rather than choose any other 'well-governed' state, such as Sparta or Crete, in which to live.

D. The Laws then enlarge on the practical disadvantages of choosing exile. They utilise on the other side of the case several of the arguments Crito used earlier in his Exhortation: the damage which Socrates' exile would do to his friends (which Crito wished earlier to minimise, see above section 3 (i)) and to himself, pointing out that as a 'destroyer of laws' (διαφθορέα...τῶν νόμων: XV.12 (53b7-8)), Socrates would not be welcome in 'well-governed' (9 (b5)) states such as Thebes and Megara. On the other hand, resorting to 'disordered and lawless states' (26-7 (d3-4)) such as Thessaly would be a public humiliation and repudiation of all his principles. Furthermore, as far as Socrates' children are concerned the Laws actually reverse the significance of Crito's point at V.6-14 (45c10-d6): on the question of Socrates' parental responsibility, death is no more of a desertion of his family than exile, and his children would be better off brought up in Athens by friends than as foreigners in a lawless state (XV.40-9 (54a2-10)).

The Laws conclude with a recapitulation of the main points of the argument, projecting the anger of the Laws against a disobedient Socrates into the afterlife where he would have to answer to their brothers the Laws of Hades.

2. Interpretation

In the arguments of A above, the Laws appear to be relying on certain assumptions which are not obvious. The logical connection between (3a) and (3b) appears to depend on a 'universalisation' argument which relates to the position of both Socrates and the Laws. The challenge to the single law (that legal verdicts must be binding: XI.20-1 (50b8-c1)) is 'universalised' into defiance of the whole system of law, which will potentially lead to the city's total overthrow (Allen, 84-5). At the same time the power of Socrates as a single individual to rob laws of their authority ('for your part': τὸ σὸν μέρος: XI.14 (50b2)) is treated as though a challenge is being offered by a plurality of private citizens (ὑπὸ ἰδιωτῶν 16 (b4)). There are different ways in which this 'universalisation' argument might be understood.[8] However, we might ask why Socrates'

---

[8]The link between Socrates' single act of disobedience and his potential to destroy the Laws might be seen as either consequentialist, ie. destruction will actually result from Socrates' single act of disobedience, or revelatory of Socrates' character, ie. his attitude to the laws is that of a destroyer. These distinctions are by no means clear in Crito, though the Laws' later arguments (XV.7-24 (53b3-d1)) suggest that it is Socrates'

lone challenge as a single individual should be treated in this way at all (see Kraut, 92). Is this 'universalisation' the only way in which the Laws can argue that Socrates is trying to destroy them, and so commit injustice against them? The other issue in A. relates to the action of the Laws. Since the city has reached what appears to be agreed is an unjust verdict in Socrates' case (the Laws never deny it) is Socrates actually bound by (2a) or (2b) which contain a proviso that agreements should be just? Of course, even if the Laws have been guilty of injustice in Socrates' case, an earlier argument of Socrates himself has established that he ought not to retaliate with injustice (1b) (section 3 (ii) above), e.g. by defying the verdict; so, if in addition (3b) is accepted, no further argument supporting the Laws case is, strictly speaking, necessary: defying the Laws is an injustice which may not be committed, irrespective of the injustice they, or their representatives on the jury, may have previously done to Socrates.

Yet the Laws clearly don't think that the argument ought to be left like this. The emphasis in (2a) and (2b) on the need for justice in the agreements between Socrates and the Laws suggests an implied contradiction between these propositions and what happened to Socrates at his trial, which, he himself asserts, produced an unjust result. But to what is Socrates presumed to have agreed? To uphold the substance of the law, or, in addition, its operation, however faulty or misguided? It looks as if the vagueness of 'agreement' in (2a) and (2b) (see above section 3 (ii)) has come home to roost!

The Laws address this problem by moving attention away from the specific verdict at Socrates' trial and attempting to locate 'agreement' at a much more general social level. The 'parent/child' analogy between the Laws and the individual citizen (*The Laws' case*, 1.B., above) introduces a new aspect to the relationship. In an extension of reference which may have seemed very natural in a fifth/fourth century Greek political context,[9] the Laws become the symbol of the state as a total political and cultural system, πόλις and πατρίς being used interchangeably with νόμοι.[10] The Laws' role as nurturers of the citizens appears to be combined with an unanswerable authority. Submission to legal verdicts becomes submission to anything the city commands its citizen to do, or any punishment it sees

---

character as a 'destroyer of the laws' that is uppermost in their minds (see Woozley, 126).

[9]Cf. 'the law' as a symbol of Athenian political identity in eg. Euripides, *Supplices*, 439ff; Thuc. 2.37. See further Ostwald, 20-54.

[10]See n. on XII. 35-51 (51a7-c3) for Plato's artistic/rhetorical manipulation of οἱ νόμοι, ἡ ʼπόλις and ἡ πατρίς as equivalents in this speech of the Laws. For the wider implications of this, see below, section 4 (i).

15

fit to impose. 'Agreement' to this broad and ill-defined framework, made at the *dokimasia*, leaves voluntary exile as the only alternative to obedience (1.C. above and Kraut, 149-93).

The contradiction is thereby avoided; the 'just agreements' of (2a) and (2b) are those Socrates entered into at the age of eighteen as part of his assumption of a citizen's role, and hold as long as he or any other citizen remains resident in Athens, irrespective of the justice of individual cases or the votes of the jurors. A high price, however, is apparently being paid for consistency; the conclusion of B. and C. seems to be that not only Socrates on this occasion, but anyone on any occasion, is obliged to obey whatever the law decides. Quite apart from its unappealing authoritarianism this conclusion does not seem to be consistent with (1a) (above, section 3 (ii)) since the law might well order a citizen to do something which is actually unjust.[11]

This conclusion has frequently been considered unacceptable, and a number of attempts have been made to modify the Laws' position:-

(a) It has been suggested that the conflict between the obligation to obey and never to do injustice is not absolute, but only applies when 'all things are equal'. When all things are not equal the citizen may have to choose between obeying the law and doing what is just, and the latter must always win (Santas, 18ff.; Vlastos, (1) 525; Irwin, 405-6). This commonsense solution certainly resolves the conflict, and Socrates could still argue on this principle that he should obey the court, if he considers that to do so would also serve the overriding interests of justice. The problem with this solution is that in *Crito* neither Socrates nor the Laws suggest this compromise. Irwin, however (see previous ref.), thinks that *Crito* does contain more than a hint of this solution, and argues that in XV (53a9)ff. the Laws are by implication conceding that if Socrates' escape would allow him to practice philosophy elsewhere (which, it is clear, it wouldn't), he would be obliged to defy the verdict of the court and escape in order to do so, since practising philosophy is, for Socrates, a command from the god which would have to take precedence over obeying the verdict of the court. To elevate this hypothetical possibility, however, into a conscious modification by the Laws of their earlier position (Irwin, 406), seems well beyond the implications of the text. Furthermore as Santas admits (26-7), if one accepts the 'all things equal' solution, it is hard to explain the Laws subsequent 'over-arguing' of the case (in B. and C. above). The 'city-

---

[11]See Bostock, 1. This is not just hypothetical; to take just one example, the execution of six Athenian generals tried *en bloc* after the battle of Arginusae in 406 BC. was an illegal act ordered by the Assembly which Socrates himself described, according to Plato in the *Apology*, as παρὰ τοὺς νόμους: (32b6), and which he publicly opposed; see also Xen. *Mem*. 1.1.18. For an attempt to minimise the illegality of this and other incidents involving Socrates, see Colson (1), 135-47).

parent/citizen-child' analogy seems to imply absolute obedience and certainly doesn't fit an 'all things being equal' solution.

(b) An influential solution argued principally by Kraut (55-90) takes the repeated phrase in the Laws' argument 'persuade [the city] or obey whatever it may order' (eg.XII.41-2 (51b4): ἢ πείθειν ἢ ποιεῖν ἃ ἂν κελεύῃ) as offering a way out of the extreme authoritarian interpretation. Not only is there room for the citizen to persuade the Laws either beforehand or in retrospect that they are wrong but, argues Kraut, *an attempt* to persuade them of the rightness or wrongness of a given decision or action, even if unsuccessful, gives sufficient moral authority to pursue or disobey the decision or action. He argues that the verb πείθειν in Greek has a 'conative' sense which does not carry the automatic implications of success found in the English 'persuade'; if one chooses the alternative of persuasion over obedience and *tries one's best* to persuade, then one is absolved from the obligation to obey.

This solution has not found general acceptance for two main reasons: 1) Unsuccessful persuasion as a basis for legitimate disobedience seems clearly ruled out by the parent/child — master/slave analogy as the Laws present it (Bostock, 14-15). Children and slaves may try to win the parent/master round to a change of decision, but cannot claim *attempts* at persuasion as moral justification for disobedience.[12] 2) Kraut's use of the grammatical category to get round the absence of '*try* to persuade' in the text has not found favour in the *Crito* context, since there is no clear way of distinguishing between 'conative' and 'non-conative' instances of πείθειν. This, the core of Kraut's interpretation, represents too uncertain a foundation.[13]

(c) A way out of the authoritarian dilemma is suggested by Brickhouse and Smith ((2), 151-2) who draw a distinction between obedience to laws that are just on the one hand and, on the other, the justice of obedience to the law, an interpretation designed to relieve citizens of the responsibility for obeying unjust laws since, according to Brickhouse and Smith, the parent/child analogy suggests that the state, and not the citizens should be held responsible for what citizens are commanded to do. As a 'child' or 'slave' of the city, Socrates need not be considered as morally responsible for unjust actions which the city initiates. There are two main problems with this interpretation: 1) it is not clear that such absolution could extend e.g. to Socrates' argument (1a) above (section 3 (ii)), which prohibits the

---

[12]It seems clear from the parallel drawn between children and slaves that *adult* children are not indicated at XII.21 (50e3)ff., with Bostock, 14, and *contra* Kraut, 91-103.

[13]See most recently Penner, who not only argues (161-6) against a 'conative' application of πείθειν in *Crito* but also questions the actual existence of such a grammatical category, which he sees rather as a 'non-completed' or 'continuous' present.

individual from doing injustice, pure and simple; 2) it is surely highly improbable to imagine that Plato's Socrates would accept absolution of responsibility for his own actions in this way.

(d) As we have seen, the core of the problem is that there is an apparent clash between proposition (1a) and the obligation to do injustice if so commanded by the Laws. This can be avoided if, as has been suggested (see e.g. DeFilippo, 257), the citizen is required to obey only legal commands that involve *suffering* injustice; the Laws, it is maintained, never require citizens to obey commands to *do* injustice. In order to defend this position it is necessary to explain away XII.42 and 45 (51b4 and 7), which refer to the citizens obligation to do things when so commanded by the Laws. DeFilippo, however, claims that this obligation is put into a context where the emphasis is overwhelmingly on suffering — being beaten, imprisoned, wounded or killed. What the citizen is obliged to *do* in these circumstances is to obey commands which may involve *submitting to* injustice, but not those which order him to *commit* injustice. This would of course cover Socrates' submission to an unjust legal verdict, would leave argument (1a) intact and would save the contradiction. It is, however, notable that this interpretation requires us to draw from Plato's text (see esp. XII.47-8 (51b9)) qualifications which are not clearly indicated. Furthermore, even if this interpretation is accepted, the problem of whether it is right to obey or disobey commands to *do* injustice still exists, and the most one can say about the Laws, if solution (d) is accepted, is that they simply do not tackle this question. And the position of unassailable moral (and quasi-religious? — see XVII.1 (54d3)ff.) authority which Socrates appears to claim for the Laws, makes it a question which needs answering.

4. CRITO IN CONTEXT
(i) Socrates, law and political activity
In *Apology* Socrates explains to the Athenian jury that his philosophising is a divinely-ordered mission which he would not give up even if the jury were to make this a condition of acquittal: 'Now if you were to acquit me, as I said, on these conditions, I should say to you, "Gentlemen of Athens, I salute you with affection but I will obey the god rather than you, and as long as I draw breath and am capable, I will not stop philosophising and exhorting you and pointing out the truth to anyone of you that I meet..."' (*Ap.* 29d1-6). This apparent conflict with *Cri.* XI.14 (50b2)ff., which emphasises the necessity of obeying legal judgements, has generated much discussion.[14] Modification of the Laws' authoritarian position in *Crito* on the lines of (a)-(d) in section 3 (iii) B above could resolve the conflict by

[14]Kraut, 13-24; Brickhouse and Smith (1), 137-53, (2), 142-4; Colson (2), 27-35; Stokes (2), 32-33.

leaving room for disobedience in *Crito*. Alternatively, it has been argued that the situation envisaged by Socrates at *Ap.* 29d1ff. is purely hypothetical: no Athenian jury would award a conditional acquittal in the way Socrates suggests; however we may interpret the obedience question in *Crito*, it is argued, this passage in *Apology* is meant simply to emphasise Socrates' absolute devotion to the practice of philosophy. He never seriously contemplates defiance of the law, and this is not the point he is making.

Whether or not *Apology* and *Crito* can, or need to be reconciled on this point, the Socrates-figure in each work presents a markedly different *persona*. In *Apology*, if Socrates' defiance is not strictly speaking of the law itself, or its procedures, he nevertheless wishes to justify his abstention from popular political activity in Athens: '...there is no man on earth who, if he genuinely opposes you, or any other popular assembly (πλῆθος) and prevents many injustices and illegalities taking place in the city, will be safe' (*Ap.* 31e2-4). In this speech he is at pains to emphasise the degree to which his moral principles inevitably put him outside, and occasionally in opposition to, practical politics, whereas in *Crito* the emphasis is on Socrates the lifelong law-abiding citizen, satisfied with his city and its institutions: as the Laws say '...Socrates, we have ample proof [continuous residence and faithful observance of laws] that we, and the city too, are pleasing to you...so emphatically have you chosen us and undertake to live as a citizen (πολιτεύσεσθαι) in accordance with us...(XIV. 9-10 (52b1-2), 18-21 (c1-2)).

Yet in both *Apology* and *Crito* Socrates starts from the same ethical base — that it is the expert in what is just and unjust, by analogy with crafts (see above section 3 (ii)), who should be the guide to living well. In *Apology* the emphasis on expertise is developed in explicit opposition to the view of 'the many' (e.g. *Ap.* 24c9-25c4), and the social implications of this position are fully developed: Socrates is the gadfly sent by the god to sting the large lazy thoroughbred horse which is Athens, and to goad its citizens into giving thought to truth and the perfection of their souls (*Ap.* 29dff., 30eff.). In *Crito* the ethical position is more systematically set out (VI-VIII (46b1-48b9)), but here the expert wisdom (which he opposes to the view of the foolish 'many') that justice demands that he should obey the jury's verdict (IX.1(48b10)ff.), is underpinned by arguments which, through the exposition of the Laws, depend on a picture of Socrates the contented citizen who has throughout his life defended the authority of the city.

Acceptance that the two *personae* are simply inconsistent with each other for reasons beyond our ken (e.g. Stephens, 6-9) comes up against Socrates' repeated insistence in *Crito* that the experience of trial and sentence has not changed his basic position one iota (VI.8 (46b6)ff.), which suggests that Plato is placing particular emphasis on presenting Socrates as ethically consistent. It may further be argued that obedience to the laws of Athens is not in fact logically inconsistent with the high level of political non-conformism demonstrated by Socrates in *Apology*. Indeed, Socrates appears to be taking the line that, in his well-publicised forays into civil disobedience (*Ap.* 32a8-e1), he was single-handedly upholding the law against either the majority of citizens (the aftermath of the battle of Arginusae) or against an illegal regime ('the Thirty', who ordered Socrates to arrest Leon of Salamis).[15] In these instances obedience to the law and defiance of arbitrary power, far from being contradictory, might be seen as essential partners.

This solution, however, depends on using what were perhaps exceptional incidents in order to make a distinction between politics and law which seems generally inappropriate for Athens throughout most of the later fifth century. The personified Laws to which Socrates, on his own admission, owes obedience in *Crito* are, in historical reality, largely the result of democratic processes, i.e. the vote of the 'many', just as judicial verdicts are reached by large popular juries[16] chosen from the citizen body by lot. How, then, is the respect owed by Socrates to the Laws in *Crito* to be reconciled with the contempt he shows in the same dialogue for the views of 'the many' who in practice both make and administer the laws?

The arguments of the Laws in *Crito* seem designed to bypass these inconvenient distinctions. Not only is the popular aspect of lawmaking ignored but the Laws seek to establish precise boundaries of influence by driving a wedge between themselves and those who administer them when at the end of the Dialogue they emphasise that Socrates has been wronged οὐχ ὑφ᾽ ἡμῶν τῶν νόμων ἀλλὰ ὑπ᾽ ἀνθρώπων ('...not by us, the Laws, but by human beings': see n. on XVI.10-11 (54c1-2). On the other hand, at XII.1 (50c5)ff. the Laws clearly wish to broaden their area of operation by minimising distinctions between themselves, the city (ἡ πόλις) and the fatherland (ἡ πατρίς), in order to advance the idea of obedience to them as the totality of civic and patriotic duty. Correspondingly, Socrates' abstention from practical politics, which in *Apology* is thought to require a defence, is in *Crito* simply ignored by the expedient of representing his legal and civic duty (obeying the laws, raising a family and serving in the armed forces (XII.10 (50d1)ff.) as the sum-total of activity required of a

---

[15]For details and discussion of the implications of these two incidents for Plato's Socrates, see Brickhouse and Smith (1), 174-84, Burnet, 173-4, and, on the other side of the argument, Colson (1), above n.11. For a full discussion of the relevant passage from *Apology* see most recently Stokes (2), 153-5.

[16]For the size of the jury at Socrates' trial see Stokes (2), 16, 168-70.

ολιτεύσεσθαι, XIV.19 (52c2)) which he has apparently in exemplary fashion.[17]

owever, leads to the more basic question of why Plato chooses to Socrates in *Crito* in this particular way. Is the Laws' requirement of Socrates being presented as an answer (or even a concession) to Crito and perhaps other friends who, as Plato suggests at V.14 (45d8)ff., failed to appreciate his radical defence in *Apology*? And does such an answer have wider implications?

(ii) Socrates, exile and the Laws
In *Apology* and *Crito* different reasons are given by Socrates for rejecting the option of exile. In *Apology* it appears that Socrates' priority is to leave the jury in no doubt about the overriding importance of his mission ordered by the god at Delphi to discuss and examine moral questions with his fellow-men. Besides being a coward's way out, exile would be inconsistent with the effective continuation of the mission, since he would almost certainly be thrown out of city after city for allegedly trying to corrupt the young (*Ap.* 37c5-e2).[18] This reason, Socrates' mission, is not mentioned in *Crito*, which is, at first sight, strange; surely for Crito, as someone supposedly long-acquainted with Socrates' teaching, this ought to represent a cogent and unanswerable defence of the decision to remain at Athens. Indeed, experience of *Apology* might lead us to suppose that the argument of *Crito* up to VIII.32-3 (48b5) ('It is not living which should be considered the most important thing, but living well') is heading in this direction. Moreover it would not have been difficult for Socrates to use this argument to meet head-on Crito's implicit definition of what course of action was δίκαιον (see section 3 (i)). What, for Socrates, could be more δίκαιον than living as well as possible by continuing his mission to the point of death? The arguments against exile in *Crito* (XV (53a9-54b2)) are, however, of a very different kind, deriving as they do directly from the Laws' arguments: a breach of Socrates' alleged 'agreement' with the city and the bad reception he will get in 'well-governed' cities as a 'destroyer of the laws'.

The emergence of the Laws as a focal point of Socrates' argument is therefore unexpected and shifts the emphasis decisively away from what

---

[17]Contrast Thucydides account of Pericles' Funeral Speech (Thuc. 2.37, 40), where discussion of the Athenian πολιτεία, while giving prominence to celebration of the rule of law, nevertheless emphasises active participation by citizens in political life (see esp. 40.2), cf. Alkibiades' ἐπολιτεύθην at Thuc. 6. 92.4.

[18]See Colson (2), p.47 n.49; Stokes (2), 175 argues that Socrates might well have subsequently continued his mission abroad on the grounds that in Plato he frequently philosophizes with foreigners; but this misses the point that, for Socrates, this activity had always previously happened *in Athens*.

has hitherto been presented (not only in *Apology* but in other Socratic dialogues of Plato, e.g. *Euthyphro, Gorgias*) as the centre of Socrates' existence: the search for truth by means of dialectical argument ('for a human being the unexamined life is not worth living' (*Ap.*38a5-6)). Why, at this point in the dialogue, does Plato's Socrates give the Laws such overriding authority?

At XV.16-22 (53c3-9), the Laws imagine an exiled Socrates approaching 'well-governed cities' (τάς τε εὐνομουμένας πόλεις) such as Thebes or Megara to tell them that 'virtue (ἀρετή) and justice are of greatest importance for mankind — *and customs and laws*' (καὶ τὰ νόμιμα καὶ οἱ νόμοι). This parenthetical addition to the customary concerns of the Platonic Socrates is odd and suggests tailoring to the context of *Crito*. On one level it is plausible to suggest that the general emphasis on νόμοι may have been intended by Plato as an answer to the sympathetic but non-intellectual patriotic Athenians (represented by Crito?[19]) who had failed to understand Socrates' conduct (see Tarrant, 75). This intended audience might also explain the prominence given to the Laws to εὐνομία (the conservative Sparta and Crete are described by the Laws as having long been singled out by Socrates as examples of εὐνομία). Socrates, Plato is perhaps implying, was no revolutionary; his abstention from practical democratic politics did not conceal a subversive political programme.[20] This speculation would gain still further in plausibilty if we can accept that in *Crito* Plato is answering the accusation of the early 4th century rhetorician Polykrates (in a lost work, known through the *Memorabilia* of Xenophon and the late Greek rhetorician Libanius), that Socrates was a 'destroyer of laws' and a teacher of Alkibiades (see Thesleff, 21n.76 and n. on XV.12-16 (53b7-c3)). Far from destroying the laws, Plato implies that Socrates gave them life-long respect, and never more so than when his own life was at stake.[21]

Yet, do not Socrates' valedictory comments to Crito (XVII (54d3-e2) imply something even greater than respect? The Laws' words, received like a mystic revelation, hum in his ears, obliterating all others. Despite their fallibility (they may be persuaded to change their minds; e.g. XII.41 (51b4)) it is hard not to identify the Laws in *Crito* with the ultimate moral

---

[19]In the course of the dialogue Plato seems to want Crito to embody at different points decidedly different personalities: on the one hand the average Athenian (Sections I-V). and on the other an associate of many years standing familiar with Socrates' teaching (Sections VI-XI).

[20]On Socrates and his associates as a species of ἀπράγμονες ('quietists'). see Carter. 117ff.

[21]Contrast the rhetoric of Thucydides' presentation of Alkibiades at Sparta (Thuc VI.92.2) who uses an alleged wrong done him by the current Athenian government as justification for aiding her enemies (see White. 120-1 n.30).

authority, the 'expert' ([ὁ] ἐπαΐων: VII.30 (47d2)) whose views will be preferred to those of the many (see e.g. Bostock, 19-20). To what in *Crito* could Socrates show greater obedience? This appears to solve the dilemma with which we ended section 3 (iii) above; *if* the Laws are the moral experts for whom Socrates is searching, *then* absolute obedience should be shown to them, just as to the expert in crafts: the trainer, doctor or farmer.

But this conclusion surely contains an element of paradox, which the discussion of section 4 (i) above has highlighted. There is no sense in which the Laws of Athens in a real-life fifth/fourth century political context meet the stringent Socratic criteria of expertise (see e.g. *Euthphr.* 5d). So perhaps we may conclude that, in placing the Laws in a historical context (i.e. Socrates' lifetime), Plato may actually be concealing another role for them, that of ultimate moral authority, a move which, while in *Crito* still in embryo and logically flawed, perhaps looks forward to later Platonic philosophical developments: the ideal state of *Republic* and beyond.

(iii) The dialogue: conclusions

Enough has been said to show that, although the shortest of the Platonic dialogues, *Crito* contains many uncertainties of interpretation. The dialogue is also not easy to place in the development of Plato's thought. The ethical argument of the earlier sections (VI-VIII (46b1-48b9)), with references to doctrines found in e.g. *Gorgias* among other dialogues, suggests a date which places *Crito* historically in the early period (see Vlastos (2), 46ff.) and yet, as we have seen, the Laws' argument may point towards later Platonic political/philosophical development of Socratic thought.[22]

Structurally, too, *Crito* diverges strikingly from the norm for Plato's Socratic Dialogues, notably in the personification of the Laws, a not-uncommon Platonic device, but unique in its extended development in *Crito*. It may be suggestive that it is in this speech too, that the characteristic Platonic-Socratic tone of ironic questioning is abandoned for a decidedly un-Socratic rhetorical lecturing style which, if it resembles anything in the early Platonic corpus, leads one to think of the 'display orations' (*epideixeis*) of Socrates' associates, for example the 'Great Speech' of the sophist Protagoras in *Protagoras* (323c-28d).

---

[22]Stokes' assumption that *Apology* precedes Polykrates' *Accusation* (for the argument, see Stokes (2), 3-4) and the conjecture (see above section 4 (ii)) that *Crito* follows it, at least suggests an order of precedence, putting *Crito* perhaps in the 380's rather than the 390's; arriving at absolute or even approximate dates is impossible. Linguistic and stylometric indicators, for what they are worth (see eg. Tarrant, 208 n.8; Ledger, 185) suggest a date for *Crito* considerably later than *Apology*.

The un-Socratic style and content of the Laws' speech has generated some recent attempts to slice through the Gordian knot of inconsistencies between the beliefs of Socrates in *Apology* and the earlier sections of *Crito* on the one hand, as compared with the Laws' speech on the other, by arguing that the Laws' speech does not actually represent the genuine beliefs of Plato's Socrates but a 'second best' ethic, a kind of civic morality which represents Socrates' only hope of persuading a Crito who clearly shows himself unable to comprehend Socrates' genuinely radical ethical position (see most recently Weiss, and also Miller and Brown). This line of interpretation reads considerably more into Crito's admission of incomprehension at XI.6-7(50a4-5) than simple Socratic *aporia*; it is at this point (Weiss, 2ff.) that the disjunction between Crito's 'yes/no' answers and what Socrates suspects are his real beliefs force Socrates to change course and abandon his dialectical argument in favour of the kind of rhetorical defence of his decision to remain in Athens which he estimates is most likely to convince Crito.

The development of this interpretation has a number of strengths: the idea of dynamic movement within the dialogue and interaction of character provides a dramatically convincing explanation of apparent inconsistencies which we have already observed in the presentation of Crito; moreover the removal of the basic assumption that the arguments of the Laws are Socrates' sincerely-held beliefs renders unnecessary the manifold attempts (see above section 3 (iii)) to reconcile these arguments with Socratic positions elsewhere.

It would certainly be unsafe to assume *a priori* that Plato intends Socrates' words in the dialogues always to represent his sincerely-held beliefs.[23] However a major problem in this particular case is how the actual detachment of Socrates from the Laws' speech is presented: such an interpretation necessarily relies very heavily on what are considered to be textual indicators that Plato is distancing Socrates from the content of the speech: for example, the reference to a 'rhetor' at XI.19 (50b7), of whose style the Laws' speech may be thought to be typical, the particular emphasis put on Crito's *aporia* at XI.6-7 (50a4-5) and the somewhat abrupt 'change of plan' this apparently generates in Socrates; on the other hand, there is also need to explain away passages which suggest Socrates' deep commitment to what the Laws say, most obviously in the simile of the Korybantic pipes at XVII.1 (54d2)ff. (Weiss, 134-40).

This line of argument has thrown up much interesting and significant detail. It may be thought, however, that particular interpretation of a limited number of isolated phrases represents a rather slim support for so radical a thesis; surely more prominent and less ambiguous dramatic

---

[23]See eg. Stokes (1), 2ff.

indicators are needed at 50a that Socrates is, at this crucial stage in the argument, relinquishing, if only to convince Crito, his sincerely-held beliefs. Moreover this thesis leaves unargued the assumption (which may perhaps generate the need for such an interpretation in the first place) that Plato's Socrates must at all costs be philosophically consistent. If one must assume that Plato's Socrates is 'tailoring' the Laws' speech in some way, a more plausible explanation, I would argue, lies in Plato's own philosophical development, and the possible audience he may, in a period well after Socrates' demise, be addressing (see above section 4 (ii)).

Plato's immediate purpose in composing *Crito* is, as with all the dialogues, irrecoverable on external evidence. Conjecturing further, however, we find the possibility of complex motivation. *Crito* purports to be an account of Socrates' last answer to the pleas of his associates.[24] There seems little doubt, however, that Plato also intended it (like *Phaedo*) as a commemoration and celebration of the qualities of his revered teacher and associate; and (as suggested above, section 4 (ii)), a particular type of commemoration, addressed perhaps to a more general audience.[25] Beyond this, Plato may also be using the Socrates *persona* to make a personal statement about his beliefs concerning the relationship between the individual and the state, including his own slightly later perspective on the reality of late fifth/early fourth century political life in Athens, and at the same time distancing himself from oligarchic individualists such as Alkibiades.

Yet however suggestive, these are all, to a varied extent, conjectures, and much is left uncertain. Does *Crito* (was it intended to) actually fit a 'last days' dramatic context? Is our last glimpse of the 'political' Socrates not of the calm defiance of *Apology* but (with whatever dramatic or philosophical motivation) an acknowledgement of the overriding authority of the state? As an example of political philosophy, the argument of *Crito* is, on the surface, quite (almost too) straightforward. But for all its apparent simplicity it remains for us an intensely enigmatic work.

---

[24]*Phaedo*, of course, presents *the* last day of Socrates' life, but by this stage he and his associates had gone beyond discussion of alternative action; Socrates is discussing metaphysical questions as a preparation for his own death.

[25]Just as the audience for *Phaedo* must have been Platonic *cognoscenti*.

ΚΡΙΤΩΝ.

[ἡ περὶ πρακτέου. ἠθικός.]

ΤΑ ΤΟΥ ΔΙΑΛΟΓΟΥ ΠΡΟΣΩΠΑ

ΣΩΚΡΑΤΗΣ, ΚΡΙΤΩΝ.

I. ΣΩ. Τί τηνικάδε ἀφῖξαι, ὦ Κρίτων; ἢ οὐ
πρῲ ἔτι ἐστίν;

KP. Πάνυ μὲν οὖν.

ΣΩ. Πηνίκα μάλιστα;

KP. Ὄρθρος βαθύς.

ΣΩ. Θαυμάζω, ὅπως ἠθέλησέ σοι ὁ
τοῦ δεσμωτηρίου φύλαξ ὑπακοῦσαι.

*Crito visits Socrates in prison.
'To-day, Socrates, the ship will return from Delos, and to-morrow you must 5 die.'*

KP. Ξυνήθης ἤδη μοί ἐστιν, ὦ Σώκρατες, διὰ τὸ
πολλάκις δεῦρο φοιτᾶν, καί τι καὶ εὐηργέτηται ὑπ᾽
ἐμοῦ. 10

ΣΩ. Ἄρτι δὲ ἥκεις ἢ πάλαι;

KP. Ἐπιεικῶς πάλαι.

B   ΣΩ. Εἶτα πῶς οὐκ εὐθὺς ἐπήγειράς με, ἀλλὰ
σιγῇ παρακάθησαι;

KP. Οὐ μὰ τὸν Δία, ὦ Σώκρατες· οὐδ᾽ ἂν αὐτὸς 15
ἤθελον ἐν τοσαύτῃ τε ἀγρυπνίᾳ καὶ λύπῃ εἶναι.

ἀλλὰ καὶ σοῦ πάλαι θαυμάζω, αἰσθανόμενος, ὡς ἡδέως
καθεύδεις· καὶ ἐπίτηδές σε οὐκ ἤγειρον, ἵνα ὡς
ἥδιστα διάγῃς. καὶ πολλάκις μὲν δή σε καὶ πρότε-
20 ρον ἐν παντὶ τῷ βίῳ ηὐδαιμόνισα τοῦ τρόπου, πολὺ
δὲ μάλιστα ἐν τῇ νῦν παρεστώσῃ ξυμφορᾷ, ὡς ῥᾳδίως
αὐτὴν καὶ πράως φέρεις.
ΣΩ. Καὶ γὰρ ἄν, ὦ Κρίτων, πλημμελὲς εἴη ἀγανακτεῖν τηλικοῦτον ὄντα, εἰ δεῖ ἤδη τελευτᾶν.
25 ΚΡ. Καὶ ἄλλοι, ὦ Σώκρατες, τηλικοῦτοι ἐν τοι- C
αύταις ξυμφοραῖς ἁλίσκονται, ἀλλ᾽ οὐδὲν αὐτοὺς ἐπι-
λύεται ἡ ἡλικία τὸ μὴ οὐχὶ ἀγανακτεῖν τῇ παρούσῃ
τύχῃ.
ΣΩ. Ἔστι ταῦτα. ἀλλὰ τί δὴ οὕτω πρῲ
30 ἀφῖξαι ;
ΚΡ. Ἀγγελίαν, ὦ Σώκρατες, φέρων χαλεπήν, οὐ
σοί, ὡς ἐμοὶ φαίνεται, ἀλλ᾽ ἐμοὶ καὶ τοῖς σοῖς ἐπιτη-
δείοις πᾶσιν καὶ χαλεπὴν καὶ βαρεῖαν, ἣν ἐγώ, ὡς
ἐμοὶ δοκῶ, ἐν τοῖς βαρύτατ᾽ ἂν ἐνέγκαιμι.
35 ΣΩ. Τίνα ταύτην ; ἢ τὸ πλοῖον ἀφῖκται ἐκ
Δήλου, οὗ δεῖ ἀφικομένου τεθνάναι με ;
ΚΡ. Οὔ τοι δὴ ἀφῖκται, ἀλλὰ δοκεῖ μέν μοι ἥξειν D
τήμερον ἐξ ὧν ἀπαγγέλλουσιν ἥκοντές τινες ἀπὸ
Σουνίου καὶ καταλιπόντες ἐκεῖ αὐτό. δῆλον οὖν ἐκ
40 τούτων τῶν ἀγγέλων, ὅτι ἥξει τήμερον, καὶ ἀνάγκη δὴ
εἰς αὔριον ἔσται, ὦ Σώκρατες, τὸν βίον σε τελευτᾶν.
II. ΣΩ. Ἀλλ᾽, ὦ Κρίτων, τύχῃ ἀγαθῇ. εἰ
ταύτῃ τοῖς θεοῖς φίλον, ταύτῃ ἔστω. οὐ

'The ship will
arrive to morrow.
A vision has told
me that I shall
live two days.'

μέντοι οἶμαι ἥξειν αὐτὸ τήμερον.
ΚΡ. | Πόθεν τοῦτο τεκμαίρει ;
ΣΩ. Ἐγώ σοι ἐρῶ. τῇ γάρ που
5 ὑστεραίᾳ δεῖ με ἀποθνήσκειν ἢ ᾗ ἂν ἔλθῃ τὸ πλοῖον.

44

ΚΡ. Φασί γέ τοι δὴ οἱ τούτων κύριοι.

ΣΩ. Οὐ τοίνυν τῆς ἐπιούσης ἡμέρας οἶμαι αὐτὸ
ἥξειν, ἀλλὰ τῆς ἑτέρας. τεκμαίρομαι δὲ ἔκ τινος
ἐνυπνίου, ὃ ἑώρακα ὀλίγον πρότερον ταύτης τῆς 10
νυκτός. καὶ κινδυνεύεις ἐν καιρῷ τινι οὐκ ἐγεῖραί
με.

ΚΡ. Ἦν δὲ δὴ τί τὸ ἐνύπνιον;

ΣΩ. Ἐδόκει τίς μοι γυνὴ προσελθοῦσα καλὴ
B καὶ εὐειδής, λευκὰ ἱμάτια ἔχουσα, καλέσαι με καὶ 15
εἰπεῖν· ὦ Σώκρατες, ἤματί κεν τριτάτῳ Φθίην
ἐρίβωλον ἵκοιο.

ΚΡ. Ἄτοπον τὸ ἐνύπνιον, ὦ Σώκρατες.

ΣΩ. Ἐναργὲς μὲν οὖν, ὥς γέ μοι δοκεῖ, ὦ
Κρίτων. 20

III. ΚΡ. Λίαν γε, ὡς ἔοικεν. ἀλλ', ὦ δαιμόνιε
Σώκρατες, ἔτι καὶ νῦν ἐμοὶ πείθου καὶ
σώθητι· ὡς ἐμοί, ἐὰν σὺ ἀποθάνῃς, οὐ
μία ξυμφορά ἐστιν, ἀλλὰ χωρὶς μὲν σοῦ
ἐστερῆσθαι, τοιούτου ἐπιτηδείου, οἷον ἐγὼ
οὐδένα μή ποτε εὑρήσω, ἔτι δὲ καὶ
πολλοῖς δόξω, οἳ ἐμὲ καὶ σὲ μὴ σαφῶς ἴσασιν, ὡς οἷός
C τ' ὤν σε σῴζειν, εἰ ἤθελον ἀναλίσκειν χρήματα, ἀμε-
λῆσαι. καί τοι τίς ἂν αἰσχίων εἴη ταύτης δόξα ἢ
δοκεῖν χρήματα περὶ πλείονος ποιεῖσθαι ἢ φίλους; 10
οὐ γὰρ πείσονται οἱ πολλοί, ὡς σὺ αὐτὸς οὐκ ἠθέλη-
σας ἀπιέναι ἐνθένδε ἡμῶν προθυμουμένων.

ΣΩ. Ἀλλὰ τί ἡμῖν, ὦ μακάριε Κρίτων, οὕτω τῆς
τῶν πολλῶν δόξης μέλει; οἱ γὰρ ἐπιεικέστατοι, ὧν
μᾶλλον ἄξιον φροντίζειν, ἡγήσονται αὐτὰ οὕτω πε- 15
πρᾶχθαι, ὥσπερ ἂν πραχθῇ.

D ΚΡ. Ἀλλ' ὁρᾷς δὴ ὅτι ἀνάγκη, ὦ Σώκρατες, καὶ

'For my sake, Socrates, I entreat you to make your escape from prison. Think what men will say of me.

τῆς τῶν πολλῶν δόξης μέλειν. αὐτὰ δὲ δῆλα τὰ
παρόντα νυνί, ὅτι οἷοί τ᾽ εἰσὶν οἱ πολλοὶ οὐ τὰ
20 σμικρότατα τῶν κακῶν ἐξεργάζεσθαι, ἀλλὰ τὰ μέγιστα σχεδόν, ἐάν τις ἐν αὐτοῖς διαβεβλημένος ᾖ.

ΣΩ. Εἰ γὰρ ὤφελον, ὦ Κρίτων, οἷοί τ᾽ εἶναι οἱ
πολλοὶ τὰ μέγιστα κακὰ ἐργάζεσθαι, ἵνα οἷοί τ᾽ ἦσαν
καὶ ἀγαθὰ τὰ μέγιστα, καὶ καλῶς ἂν εἶχεν· νῦν δὲ
25 οὐδέτερα οἷοί τε· οὔτε γὰρ φρόνιμον οὔτε ἄφρονα
δυνατοὶ ποιῆσαι, ποιοῦσι δὲ τοῦτο ὅ τι ἂν τύχωσι.

IV. ΚΡ. Ταῦτα μὲν δὴ οὕτως ἐχέτω· τάδε δέ, E
ὦ Σώκρατες, εἰπέ μοι. ἀρά γε μὴ ἐμοῦ
Your friends are
willing to run the
risk of saving you;
indeed the risk is
but small.
προμηθεῖ καὶ τῶν ἄλλων ἐπιτηδείων, μή,
ἐὰν σὺ ἐνθένδε ἐξέλθῃς, οἱ συκοφάνται
5 ἡμῖν πράγματα παρέχωσιν ὡς σὲ ἐνθένδε
ἐκκλέψασιν, καὶ ἀναγκασθῶμεν ἢ καὶ πᾶσαν τὴν
οὐσίαν ἀποβαλεῖν ἢ συχνὰ χρήματα, ἢ καὶ ἄλλο τι
πρὸς τούτοις παθεῖν; εἰ γάρ τι τοιοῦτον | φοβεῖ, ἔασον 45
αὐτὸ χαίρειν· ἡμεῖς γάρ που δίκαιοί ἐσμεν σώσαντές
10 σε κινδυνεύειν τοῦτον τὸν κίνδυνον καί, ἐὰν δέῃ, ἔτι
τούτου μείζω. ἀλλ᾽ ἐμοὶ πείθου καὶ μὴ ἄλλως ποίει.

ΣΩ. Καὶ ταῦτα προμηθοῦμαι, ὦ Κρίτων, καὶ
ἄλλα πολλά.

ΚΡ. Μήτε τοίνυν ταῦτα φοβοῦ· καὶ γὰρ οὐδὲ
15 πολὺ τἀργύριόν ἐστιν, ὃ θέλουσι λαβόντες τινὲς
σῶσαί σε καὶ ἐξαγαγεῖν ἐνθένδε. ἔπειτα οὐχ ὁρᾷς
τούτους τοὺς συκοφάντας ὡς εὐτελεῖς, καὶ οὐδὲν ἂν
δέοι ἐπ᾽ αὐτοὺς πολλοῦ ἀργυρίου; σοὶ δὲ ὑπάρχει μὲν
τὰ ἐμὰ χρήματα, ὡς ἐγὼ οἶμαι, ἱκανά· ἔπειτα καὶ εἴ τι B
20 ἐμοῦ κηδόμενος οὐκ οἴει δεῖν ἀναλίσκειν τἀμά, ξένοι
οὗτοι ἐνθάδε ἕτοιμοι ἀναλίσκειν· εἷς δὲ καὶ κεκόμικεν
ἐπ᾽ αὐτὸ τοῦτο ἀργύριον ἱκανόν, Σιμμίας ὁ Θηβαῖος·

ἕτοιμος δὲ καὶ Κέβης καὶ ἄλλοι πολλοὶ πάνυ. ὥστε,
ὅπερ λέγω, μήτε ταῦτα φοβούμενος ἀποκάμῃς σαυτὸν
σῶσαι, μήτε, ὃ ἔλεγες ἐν τῷ δικαστηρίῳ, δυσχερές σοι 25
γενέσθω, ὅτι οὐκ ἂν ἔχοις ἐξελθὼν ὅ τι χρῷο σαυτῷ·
πολλαχοῦ μὲν γὰρ καὶ ἄλλοσε, ὅποι ἂν ἀφίκῃ, ἀγα-
C πήσουσί σε· ἐὰν δὲ βούλῃ εἰς Θετταλίαν ἰέναι, εἰσὶν
ἐμοὶ ἐκεῖ ξένοι, οἵ σε περὶ πολλοῦ ποιήσονται καὶ
ἀσφάλειάν σοι παρέξονται, ὥστε σε μηδένα λυπεῖν 30
τῶν κατὰ Θετταλίαν.

V. Ἔτι δέ, ὦ Σώκρατες, οὐδὲ δίκαιόν μοι δοκεῖς
ἐπιχειρεῖν πρᾶγμα, σαυτὸν προδοῦναι,
ἐξὸν σωθῆναι· καὶ τοιαῦτα σπεύδεις περὶ
σαυτὸν γενέσθαι, ἅπερ ἂν καὶ οἱ ἐχθροί
σου σπεύσαιέν τε καὶ ἔσπευσαν σὲ διαφθεῖραι βουλόμενοι. πρὸς δὲ τούτοις καὶ
τοὺς υἱεῖς τοὺς σαυτοῦ ἔμοιγε δοκεῖς προ-
D διδόναι, οὕς σοι ἐξὸν καὶ ἐκθρέψαι καὶ

Besides it is wrong, even cowardly, to die when you might live. Think of your children and your 5 friends: we shall be branded as cowards for our share in this whole matter.'

ἐκπαιδεῦσαι οἰχήσει καταλιπών, καὶ τὸ σὸν μέρος, ὅ
τι ἂν τύχωσι, τοῦτο πράξουσιν· τεύξονται δέ, ὡς τὸ 10
εἰκός, τοιούτων οἷάπερ εἴωθεν γίγνεσθαι ἐν ταῖς ὀρφανίαις περὶ τοὺς ὀρφανούς. ἢ γὰρ οὐ χρὴ ποιεῖσθαι
παῖδας, ἢ ξυνδιαταλαιπωρεῖν καὶ τρέφοντα καὶ παι-
δεύοντα· σὺ δέ μοι δοκεῖς τὰ ῥᾳθυμότατα αἱρεῖσθαι·
χρὴ δέ, ἅπερ ἂν ἀνὴρ ἀγαθὸς καὶ ἀνδρεῖος ἕλοιτο, 15
ταῦτα αἱρεῖσθαι, φάσκοντά γε δὴ ἀρετῆς διὰ παντὸς
τοῦ βίου ἐπιμελεῖσθαι· ὡς ἔγωγε καὶ ὑπὲρ σοῦ καὶ
E ὑπὲρ ἡμῶν τῶν σῶν ἐπιτηδείων αἰσχύνομαι, μὴ δόξῃ
ἅπαν τὸ πρᾶγμα τὸ περὶ σὲ ἀνανδρίᾳ τινὶ τῇ
ἡμετέρᾳ πεπρᾶχθαι, καὶ ἡ εἴσοδος τῆς δίκης εἰς τὸ 20
δικαστήριον ὡς εἰσῆλθες ἐξὸν μὴ εἰσελθεῖν, καὶ αὐτὸς
ὁ ἀγὼν τῆς δίκης ὡς ἐγένετο, καὶ τὸ τελευταῖον δὴ

τουτί, ὥσπερ κατάγελως τῆς πράξεως, κακίᾳ τινὶ καὶ
ἀνανδρίᾳ τῇ ἡμετέρᾳ διαπεφευγέναι | ἡμᾶς δοκεῖν, οἵ- 46
25 τινές σε οὐχὶ ἐσώσαμεν οὐδὲ σὺ σαυτόν, οἷόν τε ὂν
καὶ δυνατόν, εἴ τι καὶ μικρὸν ἡμῶν ὄφελος ἦν. ταῦτα
οὖν, ὦ Σώκρατες, ὅρα μὴ ἅμα τῷ κακῷ καὶ αἰσχρὰ ᾖ
σοί τε καὶ ἡμῖν. ἀλλὰ βουλεύου, μᾶλλον δὲ οὐδὲ
βουλεύεσθαι ἔτι ὥρα, ἀλλὰ βεβουλεῦσθαι. μία δὲ
30 βουλή· τῆς γὰρ ἐπιούσης νυκτὸς πάντα ταῦτα δεῖ
πεπρᾶχθαι. εἰ δ᾽ ἔτι περιμενοῦμεν, ἀδύνατον καὶ
οὐκέτι οἷόν τε. ἀλλὰ παντὶ τρόπῳ, ὦ Σώκρατες,
πείθου μοι καὶ μηδαμῶς ἄλλως ποίει.

VI. ΣΩ. Ὦ φίλε Κρίτων, ἡ προθυμία σου B
πολλοῦ ἀξία, εἰ μετά τινος ὀρθότητος εἴη·
εἰ δὲ μή, ὅσῳ μείζων, τοσούτῳ χαλεπω-
τέρα. σκοπεῖσθαι οὖν χρὴ ἡμᾶς, εἴτε
ταῦτα πρακτέον εἴτε μή· ὡς ἐγὼ οὐ μόνον

'Crito, the only
opinions worth
regarding are
those of the wise.
Is it not so?'
'Yes.'

νῦν, ἀλλὰ καὶ ἀεὶ τοιοῦτος, οἷος τῶν ἐμῶν μηδενὶ
ἄλλῳ πείθεσθαι ἢ τῷ λόγῳ, ὃς ἄν μοι λογιζομένῳ
βέλτιστος φαίνηται. τοὺς δὲ λόγους, οὓς ἐν τῷ ἔμπροσθεν ἔλεγον, οὐ δύναμαι νῦν ἐκβαλεῖν, ἐπειδή μοι
10 ἥδε ἡ τύχη γέγονεν, ἀλλὰ σχεδόν τι ὅμοιοι φαίνονταί
μοι, καὶ τοὺς αὐτοὺς πρεσβεύω καὶ τιμῶ, οὕσπερ καὶ C
πρότερον· ὧν ἐὰν μὴ βελτίω ἔχωμεν λέγειν ἐν τῷ
παρόντι, εὖ ἴσθι ὅτι οὐ μή σοι ξυγχωρήσω, οὐδ᾽ ἂν
πλείω τῶν νῦν παρόντων ἢ τῶν πολλῶν δύναμις
15 ὥσπερ παῖδας ἡμᾶς μορμολύττηται, δεσμοὺς καὶ θα-
νάτους ἐπιπέμπουσα καὶ χρημάτων ἀφαιρέσεις. πῶς
οὖν ἂν μετριώτατα σκοποίμεθα αὐτά; εἰ πρῶτον μὲν
τοῦτον τὸν λόγον ἀναλάβοιμεν, ὃν σὺ λέγεις περὶ τῶν
δοξῶν, πότερον καλῶς ἐλέγετο ἑκάστοτε ἢ οὔ, ὅτι ταῖς
20 μὲν δεῖ τῶν δοξῶν προσέχειν τὸν νοῦν, ταῖς δὲ οὔ· ἢ D

πρὶν μὲν ἐμὲ δεῖν ἀποθνήσκειν καλῶς ἐλέγετο, νῦν δὲ
κατάδηλος ἄρα ἐγένετο, ὅτι ἄλλως [ἕνεκα λόγου] ἐλέγετο, ἦν δὲ παιδιὰ καὶ φλυαρία ὡς ἀληθῶς; ἐπιθυμῶ δ'
ἔγωγ' ἐπισκέψασθαι, ὦ Κρίτων, κοινῇ μετὰ σοῦ, εἴ τί
μοι ἀλλοιότερος φανεῖται, ἐπειδὴ ὧδε ἔχω, ἢ ὁ αὐτός, 25
καὶ ἐάσομεν χαίρειν ἢ πεισόμεθα αὐτῷ. ἐλέγετο δέ
πως, ὡς ἐγῷμαι, ἑκάστοτε ὧδε ὑπὸ τῶν οἰομένων τι
λέγειν, ὥσπερ νῦν δὴ ἐγὼ ἔλεγον, ὅτι τῶν δοξῶν, ἃς
οἱ ἄνθρωποι δοξάζουσιν, δέοι τὰς μὲν περὶ πολλοῦ
E ποιεῖσθαι, τὰς δὲ μή. τοῦτο πρὸς θεῶν, ὦ Κρίτων, 30
οὐ δοκεῖ καλῶς σοι λέγεσθαι; σὺ γάρ, ὅσα γε τἀν-
47 θρώπεια, ἐκτὸς εἶ τοῦ μέλλειν ἀποθνήσκειν | αὔριον,
καὶ οὐκ ἂν σὲ παρακρούοι ἡ παροῦσα ξυμφορά.
σκόπει δή· οὐχ ἱκανῶς δοκεῖ σοι λέγεσθαι, ὅτι οὐ
πάσας χρὴ τὰς δόξας τῶν ἀνθρώπων τιμᾶν, ἀλλὰ 35
τὰς μέν, τὰς δ' οὔ; τί φής; ταῦτα οὐχὶ καλῶς
λέγεται;
ΚΡ. Καλῶς.
ΣΩ. Οὐκοῦν τὰς μὲν χρηστὰς τιμᾶν, τὰς δὲ πονηρὰς μή;   40
ΚΡ. Ναί.
ΣΩ. Χρησταὶ δὲ οὐχ αἱ τῶν φρονίμων, πονηραὶ
δὲ αἱ τῶν ἀφρόνων;
ΚΡ. Πῶς δ' οὔ;
VII. ΣΩ. Φέρε δή, πῶς αὖ τὰ τοιαῦτα ἐλέγετο;
B γυμναζόμενος ἀνὴρ καὶ τοῦτο πράττων
πότερον παντὸς ἀνδρὸς ἐπαίνῳ καὶ ψόγῳ
τὸν νοῦν προσέχει, ἢ ἑνὸς μόνου ἐκείνου,
ὃς ἂν τυγχάνῃ ἰατρὸς ἢ παιδοτρίβης ὤν;
ΚΡ. Ἑνὸς μόνου.
ΣΩ. Οὐκοῦν φοβεῖσθαι χρὴ τοὺς

'As in gymnastics, so in questions of right and wrong: we should regard, not the opinions of the many, but only his who knows. Otherwise that within us which is concerned with

32 ΠΛΑΤΩΝΟΣ VII 47 Β

right and wrong will be destroyed: ψόγους καὶ ἀσπάζεσθαι τοὺς ἐπαίνους τοὺς τοῦ ἑνὸς ἐκείνου, ἀλλὰ μὴ τοὺς τῶν

10 πολλῶν.

ΚΡ. Δῆλα δή.

ΣΩ. Ταύτῃ ἄρα αὐτῷ πρακτέον καὶ γυμναστέον καὶ ἐδεστέον γε καὶ ποτέον, ᾗ ἂν τῷ ἑνὶ δοκῇ τῷ ἐπιστάτῃ καὶ ἐπαΐοντι, μᾶλλον ἢ ᾗ ξύμπασι τοῖς

15 ἄλλοις.

ΚΡ. Ἔστι ταῦτα.

ΣΩ. Εἶεν. ἀπειθήσας δὲ τῷ ἑνὶ καὶ ἀτιμάσας αὐτοῦ τὴν δόξαν καὶ τοὺς ἐπαίνους, τιμήσας δὲ τοὺς C τῶν πολλῶν λόγους καὶ μηδὲν ἐπαϊόντων, ἆρα οὐδὲν

20 κακὸν πείσεται;

ΚΡ. Πῶς γὰρ οὔ;

ΣΩ. Τί δ᾽ ἔστι τὸ κακὸν τοῦτο; καὶ ποῖ τείνει, καὶ εἰς τί τῶν τοῦ ἀπειθοῦντος;

ΚΡ. Δῆλον ὅτι εἰς τὸ σῶμα· τοῦτο γὰρ διόλλυσι.

25 ΣΩ. Καλῶς λέγεις. οὐκοῦν καὶ τἆλλα, ὦ Κρίτων, οὕτως, ἵνα μὴ πάντα διΐωμεν, καὶ δὴ καὶ περὶ τῶν δικαίων καὶ ἀδίκων καὶ αἰσχρῶν καὶ καλῶν καὶ ἀγαθῶν καὶ κακῶν, περὶ ὧν νῦν ἡ βουλὴ ἡμῖν ἐστιν; πότερον D τῇ τῶν πολλῶν δόξῃ δεῖ ἡμᾶς ἕπεσθαι καὶ φοβεῖσθαι

30 αὐτήν, ἢ τῇ τοῦ ἑνός, εἴ τίς ἐστιν ἐπαΐων, ὃν δεῖ καὶ αἰσχύνεσθαι καὶ φοβεῖσθαι μᾶλλον ἢ ξύμπαντας τοὺς ἄλλους; ᾧ εἰ μὴ ἀκολουθήσομεν, διαφθεροῦμεν ἐκεῖνο καὶ λωβησόμεθα, ὃ τῷ μὲν δικαίῳ βέλτιον ἐγίγνετο, τῷ δὲ ἀδίκῳ ἀπώλλυτο. ἢ οὐδέν ἐστι τοῦτο;

35 ΚΡ. Οἶμαι ἔγωγε, ὦ Σώκρατες.

VIII. ΣΩ. Φέρε δή, ἐὰν τὸ ὑπὸ τοῦ ὑγιεινοῦ and life would then be intolerable. It is true, μὲν βέλτιον γιγνόμενον, ὑπὸ τοῦ νοσώδους δὲ διαφθειρόμενον διολέσωμεν πει-

θόμενοι μὴ τῇ τῶν ἐπαϊόντων δόξῃ, ἆρα the many may put us to death: but life is not to be bought at any price.
E βιωτὸν ἡμῖν ἐστιν διεφθαρμένου αὐτοῦ;
ἔστι δέ που τοῦτο τὸ σῶμα· ἢ οὐχί;
ΚΡ. Ναί.
ΣΩ. Ἆρ' οὖν βιωτὸν ἡμῖν ἐστιν μετὰ μοχθηροῦ
καὶ διεφθαρμένου σώματος;
ΚΡ. Οὐδαμῶς.
ΣΩ. Ἀλλὰ μετ' ἐκείνου ἆρ' ἡμῖν βιωτὸν διεφθαρμένου, ᾧ τὸ ἄδικον μὲν λωβᾶται, τὸ δὲ δίκαιον
ὀνίνησιν; ἢ φαυλότερον ἡγούμεθα εἶναι τοῦ σώματος
48 ἐκεῖνο, ὅ τί ποτ' ἐστὶ τῶν | ἡμετέρων, περὶ ὃ ἥ τε
ἀδικία καὶ ἡ δικαιοσύνη ἐστίν;
ΚΡ. Οὐδαμῶς.
ΣΩ. Ἀλλὰ τιμιώτερον;
ΚΡ. Πολύ γε.
ΣΩ. Οὐκ ἄρα, ὦ βέλτιστε, πάνυ ἡμῖν οὕτω φρον-
τιστέον, τί ἐροῦσιν οἱ πολλοὶ ἡμᾶς, ἀλλ' ὅ τι ὁ ἐπαΐων
περὶ τῶν δικαίων καὶ ἀδίκων, ὁ εἷς, καὶ αὐτὴ ἡ ἀλήθεια. ὥστε πρῶτον μὲν ταύτῃ οὐκ ὀρθῶς εἰσηγεῖ,
εἰσηγούμενος τῆς τῶν πολλῶν δόξης δεῖν ἡμᾶς φροντίζειν περὶ τῶν δικαίων καὶ καλῶν καὶ ἀγαθῶν καὶ
τῶν ἐναντίων. ἀλλὰ μὲν δή, φαίη γ' ἄν τις, οἷοί τέ
εἰσιν ἡμᾶς οἱ πολλοὶ ἀποκτιννύναι.
B ΚΡ. Δῆλα δὴ καὶ ταῦτα· φαίη γὰρ ἄν, ὦ Σώκρατες.
ΣΩ. Ἀληθῆ λέγεις. ἀλλ', ὦ θαυμάσιε, οὗτός
τε ὁ λόγος, ὃν διεληλύθαμεν, ἔμοιγε δοκεῖ ἔτι ὅμοιος
εἶναι καὶ πρότερον· καὶ τόνδε αὖ σκόπει, εἰ ἔτι μένει
ἡμῖν ἢ οὔ, ὅτι οὐ τὸ ζῆν περὶ πλείστου ποιητέον,
ἀλλὰ τὸ εὖ ζῆν.
ΚΡ. Ἀλλὰ μένει.

34 ΠΛΑΤΩΝΟΣ VIII 48 B

35 ΣΩ. Τὸ δὲ εὖ καὶ καλῶς καὶ δικαίως ὅτι ταὐτόν
ἐστιν, μένει ἢ οὐ μένει;

KP. Μένει.

IX. ΣΩ. Οὐκοῦν ἐκ τῶν ὁμολογουμένων τοῦτο
σκεπτέον, πότερον δίκαιον ἐμὲ ἐνθένδε
This is the
question we have πειρᾶσθαι ἐξιέναι μὴ ἀφιέντων Ἀθη- C
to ask—is it right
or is it wrong for ναίων, ἢ οὐ δίκαιον· καὶ ἐὰν μὲν φαί-
me to make my
5 escape? With the νηται δίκαιον, πειρώμεθα, εἰ δὲ μή, ἐῶμεν.
consequences to
you or to my ἃς δὲ σὺ λέγεις τὰς σκέψεις περί τε ἀνα-
children or my-
self, we are not λώσεως χρημάτων καὶ δόξης καὶ παίδων
concerned.
τροφῆς, μὴ ὡς ἀληθῶς ταῦτα, ὦ Κρίτων,
σκέμματα ᾖ τῶν ῥᾳδίως ἀποκτιννύντων καὶ ἀναβιω-
10 σκομένων γ' ἄν, εἰ οἷοί τ' ἦσαν, οὐδενὶ ξὺν νῷ, τούτων
τῶν πολλῶν. ἡμῖν δ', ἐπειδὴ ὁ λόγος οὕτως αἱρεῖ,
μὴ οὐδὲν ἄλλο σκεπτέον ᾖ ἢ ὅπερ νῦν δὴ ἐλέγομεν,
πότερον δίκαια πράξομεν καὶ χρήματα τελοῦντες
τούτοις τοῖς ἐμὲ ἐνθένδε ἐξάξουσιν καὶ χάριτας, καὶ D
15 αὐτοὶ ἐξάγοντές τε καὶ ἐξαγόμενοι, ἢ τῇ ἀληθείᾳ
ἀδικήσομεν πάντα ταῦτα ποιοῦντες· κἂν φαινώμεθα
ἄδικα αὐτὰ ἐργαζόμενοι, μὴ οὐ δέῃ ὑπολογίζεσθαι
οὔτ' εἰ ἀποθνῄσκειν δεῖ παραμένοντας καὶ ἡσυχίαν
ἄγοντας, οὔτε ἄλλο ὁτιοῦν πάσχειν πρὸ τοῦ ἀδικεῖν.

20 KP. Καλῶς μέν μοι δοκεῖς λέγειν, ὦ Σώκρατες,
ὅρα δὲ τί δρῶμεν.

ΣΩ. Σκοπῶμεν, ὦ ἀγαθέ, κοινῇ, καὶ εἴ πῃ ἔχεις
ἀντιλέγειν ἐμοῦ λέγοντος, ἀντίλεγε, καί σοι πείσομαι·
εἰ δὲ μή, παῦσαι ἤδη, ὦ μακάριε, πολλάκις μοι λέγων E
25 τὸν αὐτὸν λόγον, ὡς χρὴ ἐνθένδε ἀκόντων Ἀθηναίων
ἐμὲ ἀπιέναι· ὡς ἐγὼ περὶ πολλοῦ ποιοῦμαι πεῖσαί
σε, ἀλλὰ μὴ ἄκοντος ταῦτα πράττειν. ὅρα δὲ δὴ
τῆς σκέψεως τὴν ἀρχήν, ἐάν σοι ἱκανῶς λέγηται, καὶ

49 πειρῶ ἀποκρίνεσθαι | τὸ ἐρωτώμενον, ᾗ ἂν μάλιστα
οἴῃ.   30
ΚΡ. Ἀλλὰ πειράσομαι.

Χ. ΣΩ. Οὐδενὶ τρόπῳ φαμὲν ἑκόντας ἀδικητέον
εἶναι, ἢ τινὶ μὲν ἀδικητέον τρόπῳ, τινὶ δὲ   Do you still
οὔ; ἢ οὐδαμῶς τό γε ἀδικεῖν οὔτε ἀγαθὸν   believe that we
                                                                       ought never to do
οὔτε καλόν, ὡς πολλάκις ἡμῖν καὶ ἐν τῷ   wrong or evil to
                                                                       another, or re-
ἔμπροσθεν χρόνῳ ὡμολογήθη; ἢ πᾶσαι   quite wrong with
                                                                       wrong, or evil 5
ἡμῖν ἐκεῖναι αἱ πρόσθεν ὁμολογίαι ἐν   with evil? Think
                                                                       well before you
ταῖσδε ταῖς ὀλίγαις ἡμέραις ἐκκεχυμέναι   answer: the ad-
                                                                       herents of this
εἰσίν, καὶ πάλαι, ὦ Κρίτων, ἄρα τηλικοίδε   view cannot ar-
                                                                       gue with the
ἄνδρες πρὸς ἀλλήλους σπουδῇ διαλεγό-   many, who think
                                                                       otherwise.' 'I
B μενοι ἐλάθομεν ἡμᾶς αὐτοὺς παίδων οὐδὲν   still believe it.' 10
διαφέροντες; ἢ παντὸς μᾶλλον οὕτως ἔχει ὥσπερ
τότε ἐλέγετο ἡμῖν· εἴτε φασὶν οἱ πολλοὶ εἴτε μή, καὶ
εἴτε δεῖ ἡμᾶς ἔτι τῶνδε χαλεπώτερα πάσχειν εἴτε καὶ
πραότερα, ὅμως τό γε ἀδικεῖν τῷ ἀδικοῦντι καὶ κακὸν
καὶ αἰσχρὸν τυγχάνει ὂν παντὶ τρόπῳ; φαμὲν ἢ οὔ; 15
ΚΡ. Φαμέν.
ΣΩ. Οὐδαμῶς ἄρα δεῖ ἀδικεῖν.
ΚΡ. Οὐ δῆτα.
ΣΩ. Οὐδὲ ἀδικούμενον ἄρα ἀνταδικεῖν, ὡς οἱ
πολλοὶ οἴονται, ἐπειδή γε οὐδαμῶς δεῖ ἀδικεῖν.   20
C ΚΡ. Οὐ φαίνεται.
ΣΩ. Τί δὲ δή; κακουργεῖν δεῖ, ὦ Κρίτων, ἢ οὔ;
ΚΡ. Οὐ δεῖ δήπου, ὦ Σώκρατες.
ΣΩ. Τί δέ; ἀντικακουργεῖν κακῶς πάσχοντα,
ὡς οἱ πολλοί φασιν, δίκαιον ἢ οὐ δίκαιον;   25
ΚΡ. Οὐδαμῶς.
ΣΩ. Τὸ γάρ που κακῶς ποιεῖν ἀνθρώπους τοῦ
ἀδικεῖν οὐδὲν διαφέρει.

ΚΡ. Ἀληθῆ λέγεις.

30 ΣΩ. Οὔτε ἄρα ἀνταδικεῖν δεῖ οὔτε κακῶς ποιεῖν οὐδένα ἀνθρώπων, οὐδ' ἂν ὁτιοῦν πάσχῃ ὑπ' αὐτῶν. καὶ ὅρα, ὦ Κρίτων, ταῦτα καθομολογῶν, ὅπως μὴ παρὰ δόξαν ὁμολογῇς. οἶδα γὰρ ὅτι ὀλίγοις τισὶ D ταῦτα καὶ δοκεῖ καὶ δόξει. οἷς οὖν οὕτω δέδοκται 35 καὶ οἷς μή, τούτοις οὐκ ἔστι κοινὴ βουλή, ἀλλὰ ἀνάγκη τούτους ἀλλήλων καταφρονεῖν, ὁρῶντας τὰ ἀλλήλων βουλεύματα. σκόπει δὴ οὖν καὶ σὺ εὖ μάλα πότερον κοινωνεῖς καὶ ξυνδοκεῖ σοι καὶ ἀρχώ- μεθα ἐντεῦθεν βουλευόμενοι, ὡς οὐδέποτε ὀρθῶς ἔχον- 40 τος οὔτε τοῦ ἀδικεῖν οὔτε τοῦ ἀνταδικεῖν οὔτε κακῶς πάσχοντα ἀμύνεσθαι ἀντιδρῶντα κακῶς, ἢ ἀφίστασαι καὶ οὐ κοινωνεῖς τῆς ἀρχῆς· ἐμοὶ μὲν γὰρ καὶ πάλαι E οὕτω καὶ νῦν ἔτι δοκεῖ, σοὶ δὲ εἴ πῃ ἄλλῃ δέδοκται, λέγε καὶ δίδασκε. εἰ δ' ἐμμένεις τοῖς πρόσθε, τὸ 45 μετὰ τοῦτο ἄκουε.

ΚΡ. Ἀλλ' ἐμμένω τε καὶ ξυνδοκεῖ μοι· ἀλλὰ λέγε.

ΣΩ. Λέγω δὴ αὖ τὸ μετὰ τοῦτο, μᾶλλον δ' ἐρωτῶ· πότερον ἃ ἄν τις ὁμολογήσῃ τῳ δίκαια ὄντα 50 ποιητέον ἢ ἐξαπατητέον;

ΚΡ. Ποιητέον.

XI. ΣΩ. Ἐκ τούτων δὴ ἄθρει. ἀπιόντες ἐν- θένδε ἡμεῖς μὴ πείσαντες τὴν πόλιν | πό- 50 τερον κακῶς τινας ποιοῦμεν, καὶ ταῦτα οὓς ἥκιστα δεῖ, ἢ οὔ; καὶ ἐμμένομεν οἷς ὡμολογήσαμεν δικαίοις οὖσιν ἢ οὔ;

ΚΡ. Οὐκ ἔχω, ὦ Σώκρατες, ἀποκρί- νασθαι πρὸς ὃ ἐρωτᾷς· οὐ γὰρ ἐννοῶ.

ΣΩ. Ἀλλ' ὧδε σκόπει. εἰ μέλλουσιν ἡμῖν ἐν-

'And suppose the Laws of my country came and accused me of doing them wrong, what should I say? Should I say they wronged me first?'
'Of course.'

θένδε εἴτε ἀποδιδράσκειν, εἴθ᾽ ὅπως δεῖ ὀνομάσαι
τοῦτο, ἐλθόντες οἱ νόμοι καὶ τὸ κοινὸν τῆς πόλεως 10
ἐπιστάντες ἔροιντο· ᾽εἰπέ μοι, ὦ Σώκρατες, τί ἐν νῷ
ἔχεις ποιεῖν; ἄλλο τι ἢ τούτῳ τῷ ἔργῳ, ᾧ ἐπιχειρεῖς,
Β διανοεῖ τούς τε νόμους ἡμᾶς ἀπολέσαι καὶ ξύμπασαν
τὴν πόλιν τὸ σὸν μέρος; ἢ δοκεῖ σοι οἷόν τε ἔτι ἐκεί-
νην τὴν πόλιν εἶναι καὶ μὴ ἀνατετράφθαι, ἐν ᾗ αἱ 15
γενόμεναι δίκαι μηδὲν ἰσχύουσιν, ἀλλὰ ὑπὸ ἰδιωτῶν
ἄκυροί τε γίγνονται καὶ διαφθείρονται;᾽ τί ἐροῦμεν,
ὦ Κρίτων, πρὸς ταῦτα καὶ ἄλλα τοιαῦτα; πολλὰ γὰρ
ἄν τις ἔχοι, ἄλλως τε καὶ ῥήτωρ, εἰπεῖν ὑπὲρ τούτου
τοῦ νόμου ἀπολλυμένου, ὃς τὰς δίκας τὰς δικασθείσας 20
προστάττει κυρίας εἶναι. ἢ ἐροῦμεν πρὸς αὐτούς, ὅτι
C ἠδίκει γὰρ ἡμᾶς ἡ πόλις καὶ οὐκ ὀρθῶς τὴν δίκην
ἔκρινεν; ταῦτα ἢ τί ἐροῦμεν;
    ΚΡ. Ταῦτα νὴ Δία, ὦ Σώκρατες.
    XII. ΣΩ. Τί οὖν, ἂν εἴπωσιν οἱ νόμοι· ᾽ὦ
Σώκρατες, ἢ καὶ ταῦτα ὡμολόγητο ἡμῖν
τε καὶ σοί, ἢ ἐμμένειν ταῖς δίκαις αἷς ἂν
ἡ πόλις δικάζῃ;᾽ εἰ οὖν αὐτῶν θαυμάζοιμεν λεγόντων, ἴσως ἂν εἴποιεν ὅτι ᾽ὦ
Σώκρατες, μὴ θαύμαζε τὰ λεγόμενα, ἀλλ᾽
ἀποκρίνου, ἐπειδὴ καὶ εἴωθας χρῆσθαι
τῷ ἐρωτᾶν τε καὶ ἀποκρίνεσθαι. φέρε
D γάρ, τί ἐγκαλῶν ἡμῖν καὶ τῇ πόλει ἐπιχειρεῖς ἡμᾶς
ἀπολλύναι; οὐ πρῶτον μέν σε ἐγεννήσαμεν ἡμεῖς, 10
καὶ δι᾽ ἡμῶν ἐλάμβανεν τὴν μητέρα σου ὁ πατὴρ καὶ
ἐφύτευσέν σε; φράσον οὖν τούτοις ἡμῶν, τοῖς νόμοις
τοῖς περὶ τοὺς γάμους, μέμφει τι ὡς οὐ καλῶς ἔχου-
σιν;᾽ οὐ μέμφομαι, φαίην ἄν. ᾽ἀλλὰ τοῖς περὶ τὴν
τοῦ γενομένου τροφήν τε καὶ παιδείαν, ἐν ᾗ καὶ σὺ 15

'They would reply: "The bargain was that you should obey us without any qualification, as our child and slave. Persuasion you might bring to bear upon us, but not force.

38 ΠΛΑΤΩΝΟΣ XII 50D

ἐπαιδεύθης; ἢ οὐ καλῶς προσέταττον ἡμῶν οἱ ἐπὶ
τούτοις τεταγμένοι νόμοι, παραγγέλλοντες τῷ πατρὶ
τῷ σῷ σε ἐν μουσικῇ καὶ γυμναστικῇ παιδεύειν;'
καλῶς, φαίην ἄν. 'εἶεν. ἐπειδὴ δὲ ἐγένου τε καὶ Ε
20 ἐξετράφης καὶ ἐπαιδεύθης, ἔχοις ἂν εἰπεῖν πρῶτον
μὲν ὡς οὐχὶ ἡμέτερος ἦσθα καὶ ἔκγονος καὶ δοῦλος,
αὐτός τε καὶ οἱ σοὶ πρόγονοι; καὶ εἰ τοῦθ' οὕτως ἔχει,
ἆρ' ἐξ ἴσου οἴει εἶναι σοὶ τὸ δίκαιον καὶ ἡμῖν, καὶ
ἅττ' ἂν ἡμεῖς σε ἐπιχειρῶμεν ποιεῖν, καὶ σοὶ ταῦτα
25 ἀντιποιεῖν οἴει δίκαιον εἶναι; ἢ πρὸς μὲν ἄρα σοι τὸν
πατέρα οὐκ ἐξ ἴσου ἦν τὸ δίκαιον καὶ πρὸς τὸν δεσπό-
την, εἴ σοι ὢν ἐτύγχανεν, ὥστε, ἅπερ πάσχοις, ταῦτα
καὶ ἀντιποιεῖν,—οὔτε κακῶς ἀκούοντα ἀντιλέγειν οὔτε
τυπτόμενον | ἀντιτύπτειν οὔτε ἄλλα τοιαῦτα πολλά· 51
30 πρὸς δὲ τὴν πατρίδα ἄρα καὶ τοὺς νόμους ἔσται σοι;
ὥστε, ἐὰν σὲ ἐπιχειρῶμεν ἡμεῖς ἀπολλύναι δίκαιον
ἡγούμενοι εἶναι, καὶ σὺ δὲ ἡμᾶς τοὺς νόμους καὶ τὴν
πατρίδα καθ' ὅσον δύνασαι ἐπιχειρήσεις ἀνταπολ-
λύναι, καὶ φήσεις ταῦτα ποιῶν δίκαια πράττειν, ὁ τῇ
35 ἀληθείᾳ τῆς ἀρετῆς ἐπιμελόμενος; ἢ οὕτως εἶ σοφός,
ὥστε λέληθέν σε, ὅτι μητρός τε καὶ πατρὸς καὶ τῶν
ἄλλων προγόνων ἁπάντων τιμιώτερόν ἐστιν ἡ πατρὶς
καὶ σεμνότερον καὶ ἁγιώτερον καὶ ἐν μείζονι μοίρᾳ Β
καὶ παρὰ θεοῖς καὶ παρ' ἀνθρώποις τοῖς νοῦν ἔχουσι,
40 καὶ σέβεσθαι δεῖ καὶ μᾶλλον ὑπείκειν καὶ θωπεύειν
πατρίδα χαλεπαίνουσαν ἢ πατέρα, καὶ ἢ πείθειν ἢ
ποιεῖν ἃ ἂν κελεύῃ, καὶ πάσχειν, ἐάν τι προστάττῃ
παθεῖν, ἡσυχίαν ἄγοντα, ἐάν τε τύπτεσθαι ἐάν τε
δεῖσθαι, ἐάν τε εἰς πόλεμον ἄγῃ τρωθησόμενον ἢ
45 ἀποθανούμενον, ποιητέον ταῦτα, καὶ τὸ δίκαιον οὕτως
ἔχει, καὶ οὐχὶ ὑπεικτέον οὐδὲ ἀναχωρητέον οὐδὲ λειπ-

τέον τὴν τάξιν, ἀλλὰ καὶ ἐν πολέμῳ καὶ ἐν δικασ-
C τηρίῳ καὶ πανταχοῦ ποιητέον, ἃ ἂν κελεύῃ ἡ πόλις
καὶ ἡ πατρίς, ἢ πείθειν αὐτὴν ᾗ τὸ δίκαιον πέφυκε,
βιάζεσθαι δὲ οὐχ ὅσιον οὔτε μητέρα οὔτε πατέρα, πολὺ 50
δὲ τούτων ἔτι ἧττον τὴν πατρίδα;' τί φήσομεν πρὸς
ταῦτα, ὦ Κρίτων; ἀληθῆ λέγειν τοὺς νόμους ἢ οὔ;
    ΚΡ. Ἔμοιγε δοκεῖ.
    XIII. ΣΩ. ' Σκόπει τοίνυν, ὦ Σώκρατες,' φαῖεν
ἂν ἴσως οἱ νόμοι, ' εἰ ἡμεῖς ταῦτα ἀληθῆ
λέγομεν, ὅτι οὐ δίκαια ἡμᾶς ἐπιχειρεῖς   To remain in Athens is a tacit
δρᾶν ἃ νῦν ἐπιχειρεῖς. ἡμεῖς γάρ σε   promise to obey us disobedience
γεννήσαντες, ἐκθρέψαντες, παιδεύσαντες,   would be unfilial, ungrateful and 5
μεταδόντες ἁπάντων ὧν οἷοί τ᾽ ἦμεν   dishonest.
D καλῶν σοὶ καὶ τοῖς ἄλλοις πᾶσιν πολίταις, ὅμως
προαγορεύομεν τῷ ἐξουσίαν πεποιηκέναι Ἀθηναίων
τῷ βουλομένῳ, ἐπειδὰν δοκιμασθῇ καὶ ἴδῃ τὰ ἐν τῇ
πόλει πράγματα καὶ ἡμᾶς τοὺς νόμους, ᾧ ἂν μὴ 10
ἀρέσκωμεν ἡμεῖς, ἐξεῖναι λαβόντα τὰ αὐτοῦ ἀπιέναι
ὅποι ἂν βούληται. καὶ οὐδεὶς ἡμῶν τῶν νόμων ἐμποδών ἐστιν οὐδ᾽ ἀπαγορεύει, ἐάν τέ τις βούληται
ὑμῶν εἰς ἀποικίαν ἰέναι, εἰ μὴ ἀρέσκοιμεν ἡμεῖς τε
καὶ ἡ πόλις, ἐάν τε μετοικεῖν ἄλλοσε ἐλθών, ἰέναι 15
ἐκεῖσε, ὅποι ἂν βούληται, ἔχοντα τὰ αὐτοῦ. ὃς δ᾽ ἂν
E ὑμῶν παραμείνῃ, ὁρῶν ὃν τρόπον ἡμεῖς τάς τε δίκας
δικάζομεν καὶ τἆλλα τὴν πόλιν διοικοῦμεν, ἤδη φαμὲν
τοῦτον ὡμολογηκέναι ἔργῳ ἡμῖν ἃ ἂν ἡμεῖς κελεύωμεν ποιήσειν ταῦτα, καὶ τὸν μὴ πειθόμενον τριχῇ 20
φαμεν ἀδικεῖν, ὅτι τε γεννηταῖς οὖσιν ἡμῖν οὐ πείθεται, καὶ ὅτι τροφεῦσι, καὶ ὅτι ὁμολογήσας ἡμῖν πείθεσθαι οὔτε πείθεται οὔτε πείθει ἡμᾶς, εἰ μὴ καλῶς
52 τι ποιοῦμεν· προτιθέντων | ἡμῶν καὶ οὐκ ἀγρίως ἐπι-

25 ταττόντων ποιεῖν ἃ ἂν κελεύωμεν, ἀλλὰ ἐφιέντων
δυοῖν θάτερα, ἢ πείθειν ἡμᾶς ἢ ποιεῖν, τούτων οὐδέτερα ποιεῖ.

XIV. Ταύταις δή φαμεν καὶ σέ, Σώκρατες, ταῖς

In your case, Socrates, the bargain is particularly binding: no one has lived more constantly in Athens than you. Even during the trial you might have chosen exile rather than death.

αἰτίαις ἐνέξεσθαι, εἴπερ ποιήσεις ἃ ἐπι-
νοεῖς, καὶ οὐχ ἥκιστα Ἀθηναίων σέ, ἀλλ'
ἐν τοῖς μάλιστα.' εἰ οὖν ἐγὼ εἴποιμι·
5 διὰ τί δή; ἴσως ἄν μου δικαίως καθάπ-
τοιντο λέγοντες, ὅτι ἐν τοῖς μάλιστα
Ἀθηναίων ἐγὼ αὐτοῖς ὡμολογηκὼς τυγχάνω ταύτην τὴν ὁμολογίαν. φαῖεν γὰρ
ἂν ὅτι ' ὦ Σώκρατες, μεγάλα ἡμῖν τούτων τεκμήριά B
10 ἐστιν, ὅτι σοι καὶ ἡμεῖς ἠρέσκομεν καὶ ἡ πόλις· οὐ
γὰρ ἄν ποτε τῶν ἄλλων Ἀθηναίων ἁπάντων διαφερόντως ἐν αὐτῇ ἐπεδήμεις, εἰ μή σοι διαφερόντως
ἤρεσκεν, καὶ οὔτ' ἐπὶ θεωρίαν πώποτ' ἐκ τῆς πόλεως
ἐξῆλθες, οὔτε ἄλλοσε οὐδαμόσε, εἰ μή ποι στρατευ-
15 σόμενος, οὔτε ἄλλην ἀποδημίαν ἐποιήσω πώποτε,
ὥσπερ οἱ ἄλλοι ἄνθρωποι, οὐδ' ἐπιθυμία σε ἄλλης
πόλεως οὐδὲ ἄλλων νόμων ἔλαβεν εἰδέναι, ἀλλὰ ἡμεῖς
σοι ἱκανοὶ ἦμεν καὶ ἡ ἡμετέρα πόλις· οὕτω σφόδρα C
ἡμᾶς ᾑροῦ, καὶ ὡμολόγεις καθ' ἡμᾶς πολιτεύσεσθαι,
20 τά τε ἄλλα καὶ παῖδας ἐν αὐτῇ ἐποιήσω, ὡς ἀρεσκού-
σης σοι τῆς πόλεως. ἔτι τοίνυν ἐν αὐτῇ τῇ δίκῃ ἐξῆν
σοι φυγῆς τιμήσασθαι, εἰ ἐβούλου, καὶ ὅπερ νῦν
ἀκούσης τῆς πόλεως ἐπιχειρεῖς, τότε ἑκούσης ποιῆσαι. σὺ δὲ τότε μὲν ἐκαλλωπίζου ὡς οὐκ ἀγανακτῶν,
25 εἰ δέοι τεθνάναι σε, ἀλλὰ ᾑροῦ, ὡς ἔφησθα, πρὸ τῆς
φυγῆς θάνατον· νῦν δὲ οὔτ' ἐκείνους τοὺς λόγους αἰσ-
χύνει, οὔτε ἡμῶν τῶν νόμων ἐντρέπει, ἐπιχειρῶν
διαφθεῖραι, πράττεις τε ἅπερ ἂν δοῦλος φαυλότατος D

πράξειεν, ἀποδιδράσκειν ἐπιχειρῶν παρὰ τὰς ξυνθήκας τε καὶ τὰς ὁμολογίας, καθ᾽ ἃς ἡμῖν ξυνέθου 30
πολιτεύεσθαι. πρῶτον μὲν οὖν ἡμῖν τοῦτ᾽ αὐτὸ ἀπό-
κριναι, εἰ ἀληθῆ λέγομεν φάσκοντές σε ὡμολογηκέναι
πολιτεύεσθαι καθ᾽ ἡμᾶς ἔργῳ, ἀλλ᾽ οὐ λόγῳ, ἢ οὐκ
ἀληθῆ. τί φῶμεν πρὸς ταῦτα, ὦ Κρίτων; ἄλλο τι
ἢ ὁμολογῶμεν; 35

ΚΡ. Ἀνάγκη, ὦ Σώκρατες.

ΣΩ. "Ἄλλο τι οὖν᾽ ἂν φαῖεν ᾽ ἢ ξυνθήκας τὰς
πρὸς ἡμᾶς αὐτοὺς καὶ ὁμολογίας παραβαίνεις, οὐχ
Ε ὑπὸ ἀνάγκης ὁμολογήσας οὐδὲ ἀπατηθεὶς οὐδὲ ἐν
ὀλίγῳ χρόνῳ ἀναγκασθεὶς βουλεύσασθαι, ἀλλ᾽ ἐν 40
ἔτεσιν ἑβδομήκοντα, ἐν οἷς ἐξῆν σοι ἀπιέναι, εἰ μὴ
ἠρέσκομεν ἡμεῖς μηδὲ δίκαιαι ἐφαίνοντό σοι αἱ ὁμολογίαι εἶναι; σὺ δὲ οὔτε Λακεδαίμονα προῃροῦ οὔτε
Κρήτην, ἃς δὴ ἑκάστοτε φῂς εὐνομεῖσθαι, οὔτε ἄλλην
οὐδεμίαν τῶν Ἑλληνίδων πόλεων οὐδὲ τῶν βαρβαρι- 45
53 κῶν, | ἀλλὰ ἐλάττω ἐξ αὐτῆς ἀπεδήμησας ἢ οἱ χωλοί
τε καὶ τυφλοὶ καὶ οἱ ἄλλοι ἀνάπηροι· οὕτω σοι διαφερόντως τῶν ἄλλων Ἀθηναίων ἤρεσκεν ἡ πόλις τε
καὶ ἡμεῖς οἱ νόμοι δῆλον ὅτι· τίνι γὰρ ἂν πόλις
ἀρέσκοι ἄνευ νόμων; νῦν δὲ δὴ οὐκ ἐμμένεις τοῖς 50
ὡμολογημένοις; ἐὰν ἡμῖν γε πείθῃ, ὦ Σώκρατες· καὶ
οὐ καταγέλαστός γε ἔσει ἐκ τῆς πόλεως ἐξελθών.

XV. Σκόπει γὰρ δή, ταῦτα παραβὰς καὶ ἐξαμαρτάνων τι τούτων τί ἀγαθὸν ἐργάσει
Β σαυτὸν ἢ τοὺς ἐπιτηδείους τοὺς σαυτοῦ;
ὅτι μὲν γὰρ κινδυνεύσουσί γέ σου οἱ ἐπιτήδειοι καὶ αὐτοὶ φεύγειν καὶ στερηθῆναι
τῆς πόλεως ἢ τὴν οὐσίαν ἀπολέσαι, σχεδόν τι δῆλον· αὐτὸς δὲ πρῶτον μὲν ἐὰν

By making
your escape, you
will endanger
your friends. And
whither will you
flee? Wherever 5
you go, suspicion
and ridicule await
you. Your chil-
dren too will suf-

fer more by your escape than by your death. εἰς τῶν ἐγγύτατά τινα πόλεων ἔλθῃς, ἢ

Θήβαζε ἢ Μέγαράδε—εὐνομοῦνται γὰρ
10 ἀμφότεραι—πολέμιος ἥξεις, ὦ Σώκρατες, τῇ τούτων
πολιτείᾳ, καὶ ὅσοιπερ κήδονται τῶν αὑτῶν πόλεων,
ὑποβλέψονταί σε διαφθορέα ἡγούμενοι τῶν νόμων,
καὶ βεβαιώσεις τοῖς δικασταῖς τὴν δόξαν, ὥστε δοκεῖν
ὀρθῶς τὴν δίκην δικάσαι· ὅστις γὰρ νόμων διαφθο- C
15 ρεύς ἐστιν, σφόδρα που δόξειεν ἂν νέων γε καὶ ἀνοή-
των ἀνθρώπων διαφθορεὺς εἶναι. πότερον οὖν φεύξει
τάς τε εὐνομουμένας πόλεις καὶ τῶν ἀνδρῶν τοὺς
κοσμιωτάτους; καὶ τοῦτο ποιοῦντι ἆρα ἄξιόν σοι ζῆν
ἔσται; ἢ πλησιάσεις τούτοις καὶ ἀναισχυντήσεις δια-
20 λεγόμενος—τίνας λόγους, ὦ Σώκρατες; ἢ οὕσπερ
ἐνθάδε, ὡς ἡ ἀρετὴ καὶ ἡ δικαιοσύνη πλείστου ἄξιον
τοῖς ἀνθρώποις καὶ τὰ νόμιμα καὶ οἱ νόμοι; καὶ οὐκ
οἴει ἄσχημον ἂν φανεῖσθαι τὸ τοῦ Σωκράτους πρᾶγ- D
μα; οἴεσθαί γε χρή. ἀλλ᾽ ἐκ μὲν τούτων τῶν τόπων
25 ἀπαρεῖς, ἥξεις δὲ εἰς Θετταλίαν παρὰ τοὺς ξένους
τοὺς Κρίτωνος· ἐκεῖ γὰρ δὴ πλείστη ἀταξία καὶ
ἀκολασία, καὶ ἴσως ἂν ἡδέως σου ἀκούοιεν, ὡς γελοίως
ἐκ τοῦ δεσμωτηρίου ἀπεδίδρασκες σκευήν τέ τινα
περιθέμενος ἢ διφθέραν λαβὼν ἢ ἄλλα οἷα δὴ εἰώθα-
30 σιν ἐνσκευάζεσθαι οἱ ἀποδιδράσκοντες, καὶ τὸ σχῆμα
τὸ σαυτοῦ μεταλλάξας· ὅτι δὲ γέρων ἀνὴρ σμικροῦ
χρόνου τῷ βίῳ λοιποῦ ὄντος, ὡς τὸ εἰκός, ἐτόλμησας E
οὕτως αἰσχρῶς ἐπιθυμεῖν ζῆν, νόμους τοὺς μεγίστους
παραβάς, οὐδεὶς ὃς ἐρεῖ; ἴσως, ἂν μή τινα λυπῇς· εἰ
35 δὲ μή, ἀκούσει, ὦ Σώκρατες, πολλὰ καὶ ἀνάξια σαυτοῦ. ὑπερχόμενος δὴ βιώσει πάντας ἀνθρώπους καὶ
δουλεύων· τί ποιῶν ἢ εὐωχούμενος ἐν Θετταλίᾳ,
ὥσπερ ἐπὶ δεῖπνον ἀποδεδημηκὼς εἰς Θετταλίαν;

λόγοι δὲ ἐκεῖνοι οἱ περὶ δικαιοσύνης τε καὶ τῆς ἄλλης
54 ἀρετῆς ποῦ ἡμῖν | ἔσονται; ἀλλὰ δὴ τῶν παίδων 40
ἕνεκα βούλει ζῆν, ἵνα αὐτοὺς ἐκθρέψῃς καὶ παιδεύσῃς.
τί δέ; εἰς Θετταλίαν αὐτοὺς ἀγαγὼν θρέψεις τε καὶ
παιδεύσεις, ξένους ποιήσας, ἵνα καὶ τοῦτο ἀπολαύσω-
σιν; ἢ τοῦτο μὲν οὔ, αὐτοῦ δὲ τρεφόμενοι σοῦ ζῶντος
βέλτιον θρέψονται καὶ παιδεύσονται, μὴ ξυνόντος σοῦ 45
αὐτοῖς; οἱ γὰρ ἐπιτήδειοι οἱ σοὶ ἐπιμελήσονται αὐτῶν.
πότερον ἐὰν εἰς Θετταλίαν ἀποδημήσῃς, ἐπιμελήσονται, ἐὰν δὲ εἰς "Αιδου ἀποδημήσῃς, οὐχὶ ἐπιμελή-
B σονται; εἴπερ γέ τι ὄφελος αὐτῶν ἐστιν τῶν σοὶ
φασκόντων ἐπιτηδείων εἶναι, οἴεσθαί γε χρή. 50
XVI. 'Αλλ', ὦ Σώκρατες, πειθόμενος ἡμῖν τοῖς
σοῖς τροφεῦσι μήτε παῖδας περὶ πλείονος
ποιοῦ μήτε τὸ ζῆν μήτε ἄλλο μηδὲν πρὸ   It is well for
you to die now, in
τοῦ δικαίου, ἵνα εἰς "Αιδου ἐλθὼν ἔχῃς   view both of this
present world and
πάντα ταῦτα ἀπολογήσασθαι τοῖς ἐκεῖ   of the next. Do
not let Crito per- 5
ἄρχουσιν· οὔτε γὰρ ἐνθάδε σοι φαίνεται   suade you."
ταῦτα πράττοντι ἄμεινον εἶναι οὐδὲ δικαιότερον οὐδὲ
ὁσιώτερον, οὐδὲ ἄλλῳ τῶν σῶν οὐδενί, οὔτε ἐκεῖσε
ἀφικομένῳ ἄμεινον ἔσται. ἀλλὰ νῦν μὲν ἠδικημένος
C ἄπει, ἐὰν ἀπίῃς, οὐχ ὑφ' ἡμῶν τῶν νόμων ἀλλὰ ὑπὸ 10
ἀνθρώπων· ἐὰν δὲ ἐξέλθῃς οὕτως αἰσχρῶς ἀνταδικήσας τε καὶ ἀντικακουργήσας, τὰς σαυτοῦ ὁμολογίας τε καὶ ξυνθήκας τὰς πρὸς ἡμᾶς παραβὰς καὶ
κακὰ ἐργασάμενος τούτους οὓς ἥκιστα ἔδει, σαυτόν τε
καὶ φίλους καὶ πατρίδα καὶ ἡμᾶς, ἡμεῖς τέ σοι χαλε- 15
πανοῦμεν ζῶντι, καὶ ἐκεῖ οἱ ἡμέτεροι ἀδελφοὶ οἱ ἐν
"Αιδου νόμοι οὐκ εὐμενῶς σε ὑποδέξονται, εἰδότες ὅτι
καὶ ἡμᾶς ἐπεχείρησας ἀπολέσαι τὸ σὸν μέρος. ἀλλὰ
D μή σε πείσῃ Κρίτων ποιεῖν ἃ λέγει μᾶλλον ἢ ἡμεῖς.'

XVII. Ταῦτα, ὦ φίλε ἑταῖρε Κρίτων, εὖ ἴσθι

This, Crito, is
what I seem to
hear them saying.
Have you any-
thing more to
urge?' 'No-
thing.' 'Then
let us act as God
directs.'

ὅτι ἐγὼ δοκῶ ἀκούειν, ὥσπερ οἱ κορυβαντιῶντες τῶν αὐλῶν δοκοῦσιν ἀκούειν, καὶ
ἐν ἐμοὶ αὕτη ἡ ἠχὴ τούτων τῶν λόγων
βομβεῖ καὶ ποιεῖ μὴ δύνασθαι τῶν ἄλλων
ἀκούειν· ἀλλὰ ἴσθι, ὅσα γε τὰ νῦν ἐμοὶ
δοκοῦντα, ἐὰν λέγῃς παρὰ ταῦτα, μάτην ἐρεῖς. ὅμως
μέντοι εἴ τι οἴει πλέον ποιήσειν λέγε.

ΚΡ. Ἀλλ', ὦ Σώκρατες, οὐκ ἔχω λέγειν.

ΣΩ. Ἔα τοίνυν, ὦ Κρίτων, καὶ πράττωμεν ταύτῃ, Ε
ἐπειδὴ ταύτῃ ὁ θεὸς ὑφηγεῖται.

Commentary

For the system of reference to the text of Crito *and other sources used in this commentary, see p.viii.*

Section I. Prologue (1), 43a1-d6

Just before daybreak C. is sitting in prison beside the bed of S. who is still asleep. S. wakes up and asks C. why he has allowed him to sleep on. C. marvels at S.'s remarkable ability, not usually given even to the old, to remain tranquil and even cheerful in the face of death. C. has come early because the imminent arrival of the sacred ship from Delos, during the absence of which executions could not take place, signals that S.'s death is near.

The Title ΚΡΙΤΩΝ [Η ΠΕΡΙ ΠΡΑΚΤΕΟΥ. ΗΘΙΚΟΣ] Crito or On Duty: Ethical.

This title and description, as with all Plato's dialogues, derives from Thrasyllus of Alexandria (d.36 AD), who divided the Platonic corpus into Tetralogies (groups of four); *Crito* is in Tetr. I, the other members of which — *Euthyphro, Apology, and Phaedo* — cover the dramatic period stretching from S.'s presence outside the King's Stoa in the Agora (*Euthyphro*) where he is to answer the ἀντωμοσία (affidavit) against him, through his trial (*Apology*) and right up to his execution by drinking hemlock (*Phaedo*). This arrangement should not be seen as indicating an actual order of composition, see Intro. section 1 (for the position of *Crito* in Plato's philosophical development, see Intro. section 4 (iii)).

. Thrasyllus may well have inherited the initial title from the Platonic period; but to this he added the subject and type of dialogue according to his own classification, in this case quite appropriately, since *Crito* is principally concerned, unusually for a Socratic dialogue of Plato (see Intro. section 2 (ii)), with the practical question of what S.'s duty is in the particular circumstances: to escape, or await execution?

For the historical background of C. and S. and their dramatic function in *Crito*, see Intro. section 2 (i).

2(43a1) πρῴ: S.'s surprise is related to C.'s departure from the daily habit of his associates to meet each morning and talk until the prison opened for the day, which was not early (*Phd.* 59d1ff and esp. d5-6). C.'s particular reasons for the early visit are revealed in 31(c5)ff. below

4(a3) μάλιστα: with numerals (and question-words requiring a numerical answer) indicates approximation: 'about what time is it?'

5(a4) Ὄρθρος βαθύς· ὄρθρος = 'the darkness before dawn'; βαθύς implies that it was still 'deep' in that period, i.e. dawn was still some way off. The phrase is used by Plato also of S. being woken before dawn by the excitable Hippokrates in *Prt.* 310a8.

6-7(a5-6) ὁ τοῦ δεσμωτηρίου φύλαξ: probably a prison officer, servant of the 'Eleven' (the state officials who ran the prison), to authorise 'out of hours' visiting, rather than a simply a porter (θυρωρός) to let visitors in at normal times, as at *Phd.* 59e4; see Burnet, n. *ad loc.*

7(a6) ὑπακοῦσαι: used regularly in the sense of 'answering the door', but, if the previous n. is correct, perhaps better to tr. 'listen' (as Tarrant, 76).

9-10(a8) καί τι καὶ: the first καί = 'and'; the second is adverbial, 'in addition'. τι qualifies εὐηργέτηται: 'he has received some small kindness from me'.
εὐηργέτηται...ὑπ' ἐμοῦ: the official has received a tip; light characterisation here of the wealthy C., and especially his willingness to use his money for his and his friends' advantage, which anticipates Section III.8 (44cff.).

13(b1) Εἶτα: expressing surprise (cf. *Ap.* 28b3): 'Then how is it that ...?'.

15(b3ff.) οὐ μὰ τὸν Δία κτλ: C. answers the implied reproach ('you should have woken me') first, and only replies to the actual question indirectly: 'Not for the world, Socrates, nor would I myself wish to be so sleepless and sorrowful [as I am, and which you would have been too if I had woken you]'. Elliptical syntax here perhaps reveals C.'s emotional state, which, characteristically, he projects onto S.

17(b4) καὶ σοῦ: καὶ here may refer back to Socrates' surprise at 6(a5): 'For some time now I have been wondering [repetition of θαυμάζω] at you too [just as you were surprised earlier]', *or* it may refer forwards, 'and furthermore...'

18-19(b6) οὐκ ἤγειρον...διάγῃς: the imperfect ἤγειρον indicates continuity of purpose, = 'I deliberately kept from waking you...' The use of the 'vivid' sequence διάγῃς, not common in Plato, allows C. to imply that he wishes that S. were still sweetly sleeping.

19-21(b6-8) καὶ πολλάκις μὲν δή...πολὺ δὲ μάλιστα: there is a sense of the increasing emphasis C. wishes to give to the train of thought: 'Yes, and I have indeed often felt in the past too...but now much more than ever...'. In C.'s short speech the syntax, and especially the particles, convey a sense of his pent-up emotion, capable of expression now that S. is awake to hear him. We also perceive S.'s unruffled calm, seen through C.'s eyes.

20-2(b7-9) For S.'s equanimity in the face of death, cf. *Ap.* 41c-d, *Phd.* 58e3-4.

23(b10) καὶ γὰρ: disclaiming an absurdity: '[Yes, of course I do] for it would be absurd...'

πλημμελὲς: lit. 'a false note' (in music) so 'out of keeping'. Tarrant, 76 aptly retains the basic sense: 'strike an odd chord'.

24(b11) τηλικοῦτον ὄντα: S. was seventy years of age (and Crito was approximately the same age (*Ap.* 33d9)).

25(c1)ff. The attitude of the old towards death is a theme which occurs elsewhere in Plato, e.g. *R.* 1. 330dff. S.'s crisp termination of the development of this theme at 29(c4) ('Quite so') in order to return to his initial question leaves the ethical basis of calmness in the face of death — that 'nothing can harm a good man either in life or after death' (*Ap.* 41c9-d2) — unexpressed at this point; but this brief excursus not only continues the portrait of S. but also foreshadows the later development of the argument at VI.1-VIII.33(46b1-48b5) culminating in S.'s declaration (VIII.32-3(48b5)) that οὐ τὸ ζῆν περὶ πλείστου ποιητέον, ἀλλὰ τὸ εὖ ζῆν ('it is not living which is of the highest importance, but living well'). Socrates (in the guise of the Laws) returns again to the theme at the end of the dialogue in his reflections on the fate of the individual in the afterlife at XVI (54b3-d2). For S.'s attitude towards death as gleaned from non-Platonic sources, see Intro. section 1

26-7(c2-3) οὐδὲν...ἐπιλύεται...τὸ μὴ οὐχι ἀγανακτεῖν: infinitive with double negative after a verb, the negative of which implies hindering or restraint '...does not prevent them from being angry...'.

29(c4) ἀλλὰ τί δὴ οὕτω πρῲ ἀφῖξαι;: S. cuts short the moralising (ἀλλὰ) by repeating the original wording of the question, asked in 1 above, with extra emphasis, implying that it hasn't yet actually been answered: 'But why, indeed (δὴ), have you come so early?'

31-34(c5-8) Further characterisation of C. in his attempt to produce pathos by repetition (χαλεπήν...χαλεπὴν...βαρεῖαν...βαρύτατ'). C. draws out the climax by alluding to what he considers to be his own exceptional affection for S. (ἦν...ἐνέγκαιμι). In reacting to what he sees as S.'s plight C. is humorously presented by Plato as always having at least half an eye on his own suffering (see sections III-V below).

35-6(c9-d1) The situation is explained in detail at *Phd.* 58a-c; the annual mission to Delos commemorated the deliverance of Athenian youths and maidens by Theseus from the Cretan Minotaur. During the absence of the sacred ship the city had to be kept pure, which meant that no judicial executions could take place. The boat had left the day before S.'s trial and was absent for thirty days (Xen. *Mem.* IV.8.2.), hence the unusually long period between S.'s sentence and execution (see Intro. section 1).

(c9-d1) οὗ...ἀφικομένου: genitive absolute: *lit.* 'which [the boat] having arrived...'. δεῖ, expressing the important idea of the necessity of S.'s death, interrupts the sequence.

37(d2) τοι δή: conceding the literal point: 'No, it is true that it has not arrived' (Adam), while going on to emphasise the imminence of the event: 'but...'.

δοκεῖ μέν μοι κτλ: μέν without corresponding δέ here denotes opinion, implicitly contrasted with certainty (*GP* 382). 'But, in *my* opinion...'.Adam's text differs here from OCT², which prefers the more idiomatic δοκεῖν...μοι ἥξει as the more likely reading from the MSS; there is no significant difference of sense.

39(d3) Cape Sunion, about thirty miles south-east of Athens, is the southernmost point of Attica, round which a ship from Delos would have to sail on the return journey. S. was to be executed the day after it arrived at Piraeus, the port of Athens.

δῆλον...τούτων τῶν ἀγγέλων...ἀνάγκη: Burnet (OCT¹) excises [τῶν ἀγγέλων] as a marginal explanation of the text, which does not strictly correspond to ἐξ ὧν at 38(d3), (note also the 'compromise' variant ἀγγελιῶν = 'messages') but the words (restored by OCT²) can stand, as reflecting in their slightly disordered syntax C.'s anxious state of mind, and, indeed, his personality; he easily accepts what individuals (including S.) assert to be the case; contrast S.'s reliance on his inner (on this occasion, divinely inspired) certainty in the following exchange (II.2(43d8)ff.).

There is an apparent illogicality in the inference δῆλον οὖν, following δοκεῖν μοι κτλ., but this naturally reflects Crito's eagerness to convince Socrates of the urgency of the situation by presenting as a clear fact what he has just admitted was hearsay.

Section II. Prologue (2), (43d7-44b5)
Socrates accepts the news but believes that the ship will take a further day
to arrive; he has had a dream, from which C. providentially did not wake
him, in which a woman addresses him and, quoting Homer, says that he
will 'come to fertile Phthia' on the third day.

1(43d7) Ἀλλ': introducing a wish, marking 'a gentle transition from the
known present to the unknown and desired future' (*GP* 15): 'Well...'.

τύχη ἀγαθῆ: idiomatic expression: 'May it be for the best', a phrase
often also found as a formula accompanying official documents:
resolutions of the Assembly, treaties etc. OCT² has light punctuation after
ἀγαθῆ, taking the phrase closely with ταύτῃ ἔστω. Tr. 'Let it be for the
best, if this way is pleasing to the gods'

4(44a1) τεκμαίρει: 2nd *sing. pres. ind. mid.*, often written (OCT²)
τεκμαίρῃ.

7(a4) γέ τοι δή: expressing certainty (δή) as far as it goes (γέ τοι): tr.
'That's what [they] say at any rate' (see *GP* 550-1).

οἱ...κύριοι: i.e. 'the eleven': Athenian officials responsible for
carrying out legal punishments and maintaining the city prisons.

10(a6) ἐνυπνίου: for the importance attached by Plato's S. to dreams, cf.
Ap. 33c5ff., where this medium, among others, conveyed to S. the divine
command of the god at Delphi, which, S. alleges, decided the direction his
life was to take (see also *Phd.* 60e1ff.). For the role of the supernatural in
Crito, see Intro. section 2 (ii).

11(a8) ἐν καιρῷ τινι: [you happened to let me sleep] 'at just the
opportune moment'; τινι, as Adam points out, n. *ad loc.*, has the effect of a
litotes (underemphasis for effect).

16-17(b3) ἵκοιο: Homeric for Attic ἀφίκοιο. The quotation is from
Homer *Iliad* 9.363, spoken by Achilles at a point when having rejected the
gifts of Agamemnon, he is contemplating a return to Phthia, his ancestral
home. The clear meaning, as S. implies at 19(b5), is that S. will die and so
'go home' two days hence. The woman clad in white may be (as Adam
suggests) 'fate' (ἡ εἱμαρμένη: see *Phd.* 115a). Diogenes Laertius (II.35)
has Aeschines of Sphettos as S.'s audience for the story of the dream (see
Intro. section 1). (For a detailed but unconvincing attempt to relate the
structure of *Crito* to the Embassy to Achilles in *Iliad* 9, see T. Payne, 'The
Crito as a Mythological Mime', *Interpretation* 11 (1983) 1-23).

18(b4) ἄτοπον: 'strange', 'out of place'; this characterises C. as someone whose imagination is fairly limited (contrast S. in following n.).

19(b5) μὲν οὖν: οὖν emphasises adversative μὲν: 'On the contrary, it seems clear to me'. ἐναργές is the usual description of dreams whose meaning is thought to be self-evident.

Summary of the Prologue
Plato's use of swift initial dramatic exchanges to establish the scene is typical of the early Socratic dialogues (*cf. Euthphr,* 2aff.); the setting of *Crito*, however, has a number of distinctive features: the early hour, which gives the meeting a particular sense of intimacy (almost everybody else is, presumably, asleep), the lightly sketched, but telling delineation of the contrasted personalities of C. and S., the latter's εὐδαιμονία = 'serenity', 'happiness' (I.20(43b7-8)) and inner certainty, the former's scarcely-contained anxiety and concern, vividly presented in the emphatic, repetitive and occasionally disordered syntax — an emotional distance which prefigures their intellectual disparity; finally the insight given to S. through his prophetic dream, a religious emphasis which returns at the end (Sections XVI and XVII) to frame, as it were, the whole dialogue.

Section III. Crito's Exhortation (1), (44b6-d10)
C. begins his attempt to persuade S. to escape from prison. C. will suffer both from losing his best friend and from the shame of being popularly thought too mean or negligent to finance S.'s escape. S. replies that popular opinion does not matter, since superior people will know the truth. In reply to C.'s next point: that popular opinion clearly does have an effect, as S.'s present predicament demonstrates, S. answers that the actions of the majority of people cannot affect a man either for good or ill.

For discussion of Crito's arguments in Sections III-V, see Intro. section 3 (i)

1(44b6) γε: here intensive.

ἀλλ᾽: preceding a command or exhortation: 'But come...'.

ὦ δαιμόνιε Σώκρατες: δαιμόνιε gives emphasis to the address, and a tone of remonstrance: 'But look here, Socrates...' (Tarrant).

2(b6-7) ἔτι καὶ νῦν: C. should clearly be seen as having made previous attempts to persuade S., as may have others. For the 'S. must be persuaded to escape' motif in Socratic literature, see Intro. section 1.

4-5(b8) χωρὶς...σοῦ ἐστερῆσθαι: most editors, including OCT² read τοῦ for MSS σοῦ, thereby making unnecessary the taking of χωρίς as an adverb, as Adam does here. Tr. '...but apart from the deprivation [ignoring Adam's comma after ἐστερῆσθαι in 5] of such friend...'.

6(b9) οὐδένα μή ποτε εὑρήσω: fut. ind. rare with οὐ μή (aor. subj. more common) giving emphasis to C.'s statement (further intensified by ποτε) '...such as I shall certainly never ever find...'

7-9(b10-c2) ὡς...ἀμελῆσαι: i.e. in the (mistaken) opinion of the uninformed. The somewhat convoluted syntax of C.'s sentence from 3-9 gives a another clue as to his state of mind and character.

9(c2)ff. For C.'s wealth, see Intro. section 2 (i). C. appears at least partly to sympathise with the incomprehension of οἱ πολλοί, public opinion, which assumes that S. would obviously escape if he had the funds; his failure to do so must therefore be as a result of C.'s meanness. It is significant that popular opinion would censure failure to help a friend much more highly than breaking the Athenian law by instigating a jailbreak. Note also C.'s concern with his popular 'reputation' (δόξω (7), δόξα (9), δοκεῖν (10)). C. operates with the language of belief and persuasion (πείσονται, (11)) — that which appears to be the case and that which people can (or, as in this case, cannot) be persuaded is the case — which, in Plato, is regularly opposed to ἀλήθεια (truth). See esp. S.'s remarks in the following speech (13-16 (c6-9)).

13(c6) ὦ μακάριε Κρίτων: possibly an ironic echo of C.'s address to him at 1-2 above.

14(c7) οἱ...ἐπιεικέστατοι: Plato's S. articulates a well-known Platonic antithesis between the ignorant 'many' and the few whose views are worth more attention. The word has frequent, but not invariable social connotations in e.g. Aristotle *Ath.* 26.1, to describe the upper or 'educated' classes; it can elsewhere simply mean 'the most sensible' or 'fair-minded', e.g. Thuc. 8.93. Plato's S. uses it to describe people, of any social status, who have superior intellectual insight, e.g. *Ap.* 22a5, where S. refers to those he questioned in the course of his 'mission' who, though popularly regarded as of less worth, turned out to be ἐπιεικέστεροι...ἄνδρες πρὸς τὸ φρονίμως ἔχειν 'more notable in respect to their good sense'. In his later work, *Republic,* the superlative is regularly used to describe the city's intellectual elite, the Guardians.

15(c8) αὐτὰ: 'these matters'.

17(d1) δή: emphasises what (according to C.) S. must see as self-evident: 'But you surely do see, Socrates,...'.

ἀνάγκη: (sc. ἐστι). As C. goes on to explain (18-21(d2-5)) one is compelled (by sheer force of necessity, hence ἀνάγκη) to take account of popular opinion as well as (καί) that of the few, since, as is self evident from S.'s present predicament (αὐτὰ...νυνί), popular opinion does matter.

21(d5) διαβεβλημένος: according to Plato's S. in *Ap.* (e.g. 18d2ff.), it was popular διαβόλη (prejudice, misrepresentation) of him and what he stood for which condemned him, thereby making C.'s point, as he sees it.

22-24(d6-8) εἰ γὰρ ὤφελον: formula of wishing that what the previous speaker has said could come true (*GP* 93). S. is ironically wishing that the many *could* have the power to harm him, since this would entail also the power to do good.

ἵνα οἷοί...ἦσαν: ἵνα + imperf. indic. indicates a purpose that is not realisable: Tr. '[I wish ...that the many were able to accomplish the greatest evils] so that they might be capable also of the greatest good.'

24-26(d8-10) An expression of a key Socratic doctrine that virtue is knowledge: the many (and so, the ignorant) are powerless to act either for great good or great ill since the only person who can harm others or do them good is the person who has knowledge (see *Ap.* 30c2ff.). This belief, worked out in more detail in *Grg.* 466c-68e, is not expanded further here, but foreshadows the development of the Socratic doctrine of expertise below (Sections VI-VIII (46b1-48b9).

26(d10) ποιοῦσι...τύχωσι: 'they do whatever they chance to do', i.e. what they achieve is more by luck than judgement, since their ignorance prevents them from being able to fulfil their intention of doing good or ill. For discussion of the meaning of this phrase, see Penner 153-5.

Section IV. Crito's Exhortation (2), (44e1-45c5)
C. goes on to clear up what he sees as further possible objections: that S. may be worrying about the unpleasant consequences for C. and his friends of having aided S.'s escape: that they may be forced to forfeit money and property. When S. admits that he has thought about such matters, C. points out that there are foreigners staying in Athens, among them Simmias of Thebes, who would also be willing to pay for S.'s escape. S. would be welcome abroad, e.g. in Thessaly, where C. has friends who would protect him.

1(44e1) ταῦτα μὲν δή...ἐχέτω: μὲν δή indicates that the speaker considers that this line of argument should be concluded and that they should get on to other matters (τάδε δέ): 'Well, let that be so; but, Socrates, just tell me this'. Just as S. cut short C.'s earlier moralising about old age and attitudes to death (Section 1.29 (43c4) above), so here C. abruptly terminates the considerable potential of the current theme for philosophical development; he appears, somewhat hastily, to accept S.'s argument, but it is really as if he wishes to 'head off' S. and make his exhortation on strictly pragmatic grounds. But as we see shortly (Section VI ff.), the diversion is only temporary; S. will not tolerate the abandonment of philosophical principle.

2(e2) ἆρά γε μὴ: 'Can it possibly be that...?' (*GP* 47-8).

4(e3) οἱ συκοφάνται: in a state where prosecution in public cases (γραφή) was largely left to the private citizen, συκοφάνται (= 'informers'; *literally* 'fig denouncers' — but derivation and original meaning obscure) made money either by prosecuting in order to gain financial rewards, or by blackmailing someone who wished to avoid prosecution.

5-6(e4) ὡς...ἐκκλέψασιν: 'on the grounds that we stole you away'; ὡς + *part.* gives the reason for the prosecution.

5-8(e4-6) The συκοφάνται would cause trouble by initiating a prosecution against C., or his friends for aiding the escape of a condemned criminal, with severe financial penalties or worse if they are found guilty.

8(e6) ἄλλο...παθεῖν: 'euphemistic for death or exile' (Adam).

9(45a1-2) ἡμεῖς γάρ που δίκαιοί ἐσμεν: C. is asserting that he and his friends would be 'just' (behaving justly or rightly) in running the risk of prosecution. The implied paradox foreshadows the main themes of the dialogue — who is to be the judge of what is just (VII.25(47c8)ff.) and whether, from S.'s point of view, breaking the law in the way C. urges is in fact just (XI.8(50a6)ff.). On the values expressed and implied here, see Intro. section 3 (i) and for the meaning of τὸ δίκαιον, see Intro. section 3 (ii) n.5.

11(a3) ἀλλ': expresses 'a transition from arguments for action to a statement of the action required' (*GP* 14), 'Come now...'.

14(a6) μήτε τοίνυν...φοβοῦ: τοίνυν shows C. directly answering what he thinks is S.'s concern (*GP* 569): 'Well then, don't be frightened of these things'. C. immediately interprets S.'s thoughtfulness as fear of the consequences for C. and his friends (20(b2-3) below), which S.'s subsequent argument shows is far from his thoughts. Wrongly supposing from 12-13 (a4-5) that S. is on his wavelength, C. redoubles his efforts to meet what he mistakenly imagines are S.'s scruples.

Strictly speaking μήτε ('neither') requires an answering μήτε ('nor'), but this is not picked up until the repetition of the phrase at 24(b6)f., the intervening dislocation of syntax again reflecting C.'s anxious train of thought: he breaks off in 14 (a6 — see following note) to deal with what he feels are more pressing matters — S.'s concerns about money!

καὶ γάρ: C. is struck by another thought, as it were, which he expresses parenthetically:' — and in point of fact...'.

15(a7) τινές: S.'s friends and associates.

16(a8) ἔπειτα: 'furthermore'.

17(a8-9) τούτους τοὺς συκοφάντας: τούτους signifies contempt. For C.'s personal problems with συκοφάνται, see Xen. *Mem.* II.9., and Intro. section 2 (i).

18(a9) ἐπ' αὐτούς: = 'against (i.e. to settle) them'.

19(b1) τὰ ἐμὰ χρήματα: for a joke made by Plato's S. about C.'s reputed money-making capacity, see *Euthd.* 304c3.

20(b2) ἐμοῦ κηδόμενος: '...on account of the danger from the συκοφάνται, not of course for the loss of the money'. (Adam). I am not so sure about this; the danger may well have been S.'s concern, but C.'s assumption that S.'s main worry was the expenditure of money fits the context and is consistent with his total failure to understand S.'s character and motives.

20-1(b3) ξένοι οὗτοι: C. in his excited state speaks as though they were present beside him (they are no doubt supposed to be coming to the prison shortly, as Burnet remarks, n. *ad loc.*). Foreigners could not be harmed by συκοφάνται, because they had no Athenian property to lose, and no need to stay in Athens if trouble broke.

22(b4) ἐπ' αὐτο τοῦτο: 'for this very purpose'.

22-3(b4-5) Simmias and Kebes: Thebans, and young followers of Socrates, formerly of Philolaos the Pythagorean while he was in Thebes. They are named in *Phd.* 59b as among the foreigners present on S.s last day of life, and their Pythagorean interest in the fate of the soul in the afterlife is reflected in the prominent role they are assigned in that dialogue.

23(b5-6) καὶ ἄλλοι πολλοὶ πάνυ: for the 'international' spread of S.'s friends and followers, see *Phd.* 57aff., and Intro. section 1.

24(b6) μήτε ταῦτα φοβούμενος: C. resumes the construction from 14(a6) above, answered by μήτε ('nor') in the following line.

25(b7) ὅ ἔλεγες ἐν τῷ δικαστηρίῳ: a reference to a theme in S.'s defence speech, the futility of proposing the penalty of exile to other πόλεις (*Ap.* 37d); though the emphasis in *Ap.* is different: there S. suggests that he could find plenty to do in his accustomed manner, but was likely to be prevented by the authorities.

26(b8) ὅτι οὐκ ἂν ἔχοις...χρῷο σαυτῷ: literally: '...that you would not have, [in going into exile, the knowledge] how you should use yourself' (χρῷο = optative after optative ἂν ἔχοις).

27(c1) πολλαχοῦ...ἄλλοσε...ὅποι ἂν ἀφίκῃ: ἄλλοσε goes oddly with πολλαχοῦ: we can only assume that if the text is correct, it has been influenced by the following ὅποι: literal tr. 'For in many places and to wherever else you may come...'.

28(c2) S. had already declined an invitation to other places, e.g. the court of Archelaos of Macedon (Aristotle, *Rhet.* 1398a24). For other invitations, see D.L.II.25. Philosophical connections with Thessalians are indicated from S.'s friendship with the young Meno (*Meno* 70bff.).

Section V. Crito's Exhortation (3), (45c6-46a9)
Finally C. goes on to the attack, and attempts to argue that S.'s decision is not consistent with acting rightly: his choice of death will be an irresponsible betrayal of his children who will suffer all the disadvantages of being fatherless; C. then returns to the theme with which he started: that S.'s failure to act decisively to prevent the course of events which has led to his present position will reflect badly on the courage and enterprise of C. and his friends. He concludes with an short peroration, urging S. to act for all their sakes.

1(45c6) ἔτι...οὐδὲ δίκαιόν: C. believes that S.'s proposed course of action is 'not even right [quite apart from what people may think]'. Having termed himself and his friends δίκαιοι (section IV.9(a1) above), C. now uses this value word against S. It is clear from what follows in what sense C. is using it: by allowing himself to be executed, S. is failing in his obligations, both to himself by not defending himself against his enemies, and to his friends by showing himself heedless of their reputation. C. seems unaware of the element of paradox in describing S. as contemplating an action which is not δίκαιον, by virtue of actions which, in another sense of the word, must be termed δίκαιον (i.e. law-abiding). Once again the central dilemma of the dialogue is implicitly foreshadowed (see Intro. section 3 (i)).

2(c6) σαυτὸν προδοῦναι: C. seems to be arguing that S.'s. 'forsaking himself' is parallel to forsaking his children (7-8 (c9-d1) below), as both being οὐ δίκαιον. A striking illustration of the popular Greek assumption that one had an obligation to defend oneself and one's dependants against personal enemies, inside or outside the law (see Dover, 180-4).

3(c7)ff. C. elaborates on his value-judgement in 1(c6) above. S.'s failure to defend himself from his enemies (see previous note) makes him deficient in the basic ἀρετή (excellence) required of an Athenian citizen (see below 16(d8)). Adam thinks that C.'s reproach of 'self abandonment' refers specifically to S.'s failure to live up to the words of *Ap.* 28ff., where he had emphasised the necessity of 'remaining at his post' in pursuing his philosophical mission. C., however, doesn't really show much sign of caring about S.'s mission; his criticism is more general: S. is simply not behaving as a normal Athenian citizen should.

σπεύδεις: S. 'eagerly seeks' his own destruction as wholeheartedly as his enemies, as C. sees it. For the tradition that S. saw death as a way of avoiding the unpleasantness of old age, see Xen. *Ap.* 5-8.

7(c10) υἱεῖς: S. had three sons, one a youth Lamprokles (Xen. *Mem.* II.2.1) and two still small (*Phd.* 116b1), Sophroniskos and Menexenos. Plato's S. commends their moral education to the jury in his final words of defence in *Ap.* 41e.

8(d1) ἐκθρέψαι...ἐκπαιδεῦσαι: the emphasis on the thoroughness of the process (ἐκ-) is very much to the point, as C. would see it, in view of S.'s emphasis on moral development through education, e.g. in *Laches.*

9(d2) οἰχήσει καταλιπών: 'you will depart [from this world], leaving them in the lurch'.

τὸ σὸν μέρος: emphasises what C. regards as S.'s selfishness: 'as far as you are concerned'. This phrase recurs at XI.14 (50b2).

11-12(d4) ἐν ταῖς ὀρφανίαις: for the legal disadvantages of young children left as orphans (i.e. fatherless) see MacDowell, 93-5.

13(d5) ξυνδιαταλαιπωρεῖν: a word only found here in extant Greek literature = 'endure hardship together (ξύν — in partnership with the children) through to the end (διά)'.

15-16(d7-8) ἀγαθός...ἀνδρεῖος...ἀρετῆς: C. gives all these strong value terms their conventional significance. S.'s failure to measure up to an acceptable standard of behaviour is such as to cause his friends shame (18(e1)).

φάσκοντά γε δή: γε is given sarcastic emphasis by δή- 'since you *say* at least that you have devoted yourself...'.(ἐπιμελεῖσθαι is the standard Platonic word for S.'s devotions, e.g. *La.* 187a4). There is an irony here of which C. is apparently not aware (as a disciple of S. surely he should be!) — that life-long devotion to ἀρετή (as S. understands it) is exactly what is preventing him from satisfying C. by conforming to standards of *conventional* ἀρετή (see *Ap.* 30b2-4).

18(e1) δόξῃ: see above, note on Section III.9(44c2)ff.

19(e2) ἀνανδρίᾳ: C. moves from the direct moral argument back to the theme with which the Exhortation started, concern with how S.'s conduct and situation reflect in popular estimation (δόξα) on C. and his friends.

20(e3)ff. καὶ ἡ εἴσοδος...καὶ αὐτὸς ὁ ἀγὼν: all parallel with (and expanding upon) ἅπαν τὸ πρᾶγμα (19(e1-2)).

20-1(e3) εἴσοδος τῆς δίκης: i.e. the pre-trial formalities, principally the ἀνάκρισις (preliminary hearing), at which point S. could doubtless have avoided a trial by quietly leaving Athens (see *Ap.* 29c2ff.).

εἰσῆλθες: εἰσῆλθεν is the reading of the Bodleian MS, accepted by OCT², making a more idiomatic phrase, and supplying a subject for ἡ εἴσοδος: '...the entry into court, how (the case) was introduced when it need not have been...'; hence the ἐξόν clause.

21-2(e4) ὁ ἀγων...ὡς ἐγένετο: this description would fit Plato's *Apology*, in which S. refused to conduct a conventional defence, instead producing what amounted to a justification of his life and conduct. C. implies S.'s μεγαληγορία (lofty, arrogant tone) as described by Xenophon in his *Apology* (*Ap.*1).

23(e5) τὸ τελευταῖον δὴ τουτί: 'this *denouement*', i.e. the situation they are in at that moment (τὸ τελευταῖον might also be taken adverbially; 'to crown it all' (Burnet)).

ὥσπερ κατάγελως τῆς πράξεως: 'to complete the farce, as it were...'. ἡ εἴσοδος (20 (e3: entrance of a theatre stage and a court of justice), and ὁ ἀγών (21(e4: law-suit and acting), suggest that C. is here introducing a metaphor from the stage, in which S.'s legal process has become, through his own actions, not tragedy but a κατάγελως (see Adam n. *ad loc.*).

23-4(e6-46a1) κακία...δοκεῖν: in the rising tide of his vehemence C. loses his way in the syntax of the long straggling sentence starting at 17(d9);

δοκεῖν (24(46a1)), is probably parallel with πεπρᾶχθαι (20(e2)) after μὴ δόξῃ (18(e1)). '[I am ashamed, in fear that it may seem]...that through a certain cowardice and unmanliness on our part the whole affair [ἅπαν τὸ πρᾶγμα] may seem to have slipped out of our hands' or, assuming (with Adam) σέ as the subject of διαπεφευγέναι: '...you may be thought to have given us the slip...'.

26-8(a3-4) ταῦτα...ἡμίν: The beginning of the formal close of the Exhortation; with ἅμα τῷ κακῷ...αἰσχρὰ, C. neatly combines the two main types of appeal he has made in the course of his speech: to self-interest and to morality. σοί καὶ ἡμῖν reiterates the ever-present underlying theme of C.'s speech — the effect S.'s death will have on his own reputation and that of S.'s other friends: 'we are all in this together'.

28(a4)ff. C. reiterates the need for βουλή (NB. the force of the perfect infinitive βεβουλεῦσθαι has particular effect here: they should by now be acting on decisions already made).

ἀλλὰ: see n. on IV.11(45a3) above.

30(a6) τῆς...ἐπιούσης νυκτὸς: C. evidently does not believe in, or it suits his argument not to appear to believe in, S.'s dream, and supposes that the execution will still take place the following day.

32-3(a7-9) C.'s final sentences become shorter and simpler, and his conclusion repeats the words of Section IV.11(45a3), but with extra emphasis.

C.'s Exhortation (summary of Sections III-V)
Style
The conclusion of C.'s more or less uninterrupted speech marks the end of the first part of *Crito*. Despite having an audience of one, C. brings all his emotional and persuasive powers to bear in the construction of what amounts, in rhetorical terminology, to a formal παραίνεσις ('exhortation'), by deploying a number of rhetorical devices:-
• verbal repetitions in the speech mark the formal boundaries of the peroration, e.g. ἔτι καὶ νῦν ἐμοὶ πείθου / ἀλλ᾽ ἐμοὶ πείθου καὶ μὴ ἄλλως ποίει / πείθου μοι καὶ μηδαμῶς ἄλλως ποίει (III.2(44b7) / IV.11(45a3) / V.33(46a8)); οἷος τ᾽ ὢν σῴζειν /οἵτινές σε οὐχὶ ἐσώσαμεν (III.7-8(44b10-c1) / V.24(46a1); οἷον τε ὂν καὶ δυνατόν / ἀδύνατον καὶ οὐκέτι οἷόν τε (V.25-6(46a2) /V.31-2(46a7)).
• the style is further heightened with rhetorical questions, e.g. III.9-10(44c2-3) and IV.2(44e2)ff. and many direct imperatives/prohibitions e.g. IV.14(45a6); V.27,28(46a3-4). There is also the sense that C. is consciously deploying arguments in formal sequence, e.g.

ταῦτα...ἐχέτω...τάδε δέ (1(44e1): ἔπειτα...ἔπειτα καὶ (IV.16-19(45a8-b2)); ἔτι δέ (V.1(45c6)) in order to impress S. with the cumulative weight of his case.

C. therefore often tries to reinforce his point by repetition; but within the formal rhetoric there is also evidence of a typically Platonic characterisation by style (ἠθοποιία); straggling sentences with loose syntax present C. as someone losing his way in his struggle to convince (III.3-9(44b7-c2)) which towards the end suggest exasperation verging on real anger (V.14-26(45d7-46a3)); for C.'s occasional sarcasm see e.g. n. on V.15-16(45d7-8)).

Content

The basis of all C.'s arguments is concern for popular opinion — what people will assume, what will *seem to be* the case. There is a great frequency of words of the δοκ- root; (III.7(44b10), 9(c2), 18(d2), V.1(45c6), 7(c10), 14(d6), 18(e1), 24(46a1)); this extends into C.'s appeal to τὸ δίκαιον, where (V.1) he gives it as *his opinion* that S., quite apart from arguments from personal interest, will not be acting rightly in remaining in Athens; as an Athenian citizen S. should be defending himself and his family and friends against his enemies, not abandoning them (see Intro. section 3 (i)).

Yet in dramatic terms Plato undermines C.'s παραίνεσις from the start: the two brief interventions from S. (III.13-16(44c6-9) and 22-26(d6-10)) foreshadow his subsequent demolition (in S.'s own terms, at least) of C.'s case; moreover C.'s misunderstanding of the third intervention, the reason for S.'s 'taking thought' at IV.12-14(45a4-6) — his assumption that S. must be as worried about the financial angle as *he* is — introduces an underlying note of humour at C.'s expense. How could a close associate be so wrong about S.'s attitude to money? But plausibility may be sacrificed here; C.'s apparent ignorance of the most basic traits of S.'s character does not quite tally with his status as a long-term close associate.

It will shortly become evident, however, that C.'s 'popular' view of S.'s position is not simply a foil for S.'s subsequent rebuttal, but contains tensions and omissions which foreshadow the later argument: for example, it is notable that the very argument which C. passes over in silence as, presumably, having no weight whatever with him — that it might be δίκαιον to obey a formal legal decision of an Athenian court, or even to disobey it if considered ἄδικον (see below, XI.22-3(50c1-2)) — becomes subsequently of some significance.

C.'s arguments also contain interest as possible evidence of further strands in the fifth and fourth century tradition relating to S.'s trial and execution and, in particular, possible evidence of a failure among some of his supporters to understand, or be sympathetic to his unconventional behaviour at his trial (see esp. V.17-26(45d9-46a4) and Intro. section 4 (ii)).

Section VI. Socrates' reply: review of basic Socratic principles (1), (46b1-47a11)

Socrates begins his reply to C. by stating that a decision will have to be made on principles which he has long held: changes in principle cannot be made simply because external circumstances have altered. With immediate relevance to C.'s argument about public opinion, it is surely the case that a long-held view, that some opinions are to be preferred to others, must still hold good, the opinions of the wise being preferred to those of the foolish.

For discussion of the arguments of sections VI-VIII, see Introduction, section 3 (ii).

1(46b1) ᾿Ω φίλε Κρίτων: unusual initial position of address signifies the emphatic nature S.'s reply.

προθυμία: cf. III.12(44c5) above. A lightly ironic reference to C.'s style of address, the humorous allusion possibly continued in πολλοῦ ἀξία: 'worth a lot (of money)'.

2(b2) ὀρθότητος: S. here introduces a new concept into the debate, directly opposed to δόξα: (irrespective of public opinion) is C. *right* or not (ὀρθότης has the sense of 'straight' or 'correct')? Misdirected enthusiasm is bad in direct proportion to its intensity (ὅσῳ...τοσούτῳ).

4(b3) σκοπεῖσθαι: = 'consider (pursue an inquiry)' a common term in Plato to indicate philosophical investigation; here its emphatic position makes a clear (reproving?) contrast with προθυμία. Clear-headed investigation of the question should be preferred to enthusiasm, however well-intentioned.

4-5(b3-4) εἴτε...πρακτέον εἴτε μή: C. could doubtless have retorted at this point that this is precisely what his παραίνεσις was aiming to do; but ὀρθότητος and σκοπεῖσθαι (2(46b2)and 4(b3) above) indicate that S. wishes his practical decision to be based on principles and not on C.'s estimate of public opinion.

5-6(b4) οὐ μόνον νῦν: against all MSS, inscriptional evidence (on a bust of Socrates: IG XIV 318 no.1214) suggests the reading οὐ νῦν πρῶτον, adopted by Burnet and OCT². The MSS corruption is explained by Burnet, n. *ad loc.* Literal tr. '...not now for the first time but always I have been the kind of person to...'

ἀεὶ: We know almost nothing of the history of S.'s intellectual development. If we believe *Ap.* 21bff., S.'s 'mission' to question individuals in a quest for the truth should be dated from Chaerephon's visit to the Delphic oracle, at some time during the Peloponnesian war. Aristophanes' *Clouds*, (423 BC., revised 418-416) in associating S. with the Sophists, notoriously gives a widely differing picture of his objectives and methods from that suggested here.

6-7(b5) τῶν ἐμῶν...τῷ λόγῳ: here λόγος = 'line of argument', almost personified as the most trustworthy of S.'s 'friends'. Tarrant, (tr. and n.21 (208)) suggests that this anticipates the much more elaborate later personification of the Laws. πείθεσθαι...τῷ λόγῳ answers C.'s πείθου μοι (V.33(46a8)), just as τῶν ἐμῶν (6(b5)) recalls IV.2-3(44b2-3 ἐμοῦ...καὶ τῶν ἄλλων ἐπιτηδείων). S. will put his trust in argument, not in C. or his friends.

8(b6) τοὺς δὲ λόγους: OCT² reads δή: 'you may be assured...'

9(b7) ἔλεγον: note the force of the imperfect here; S. *habitually* developed these lines of argument. It is a moot point how far an S. 'expounding the best line of argument' is consistent with the S. of the 'aporetic' dialogues, conversations in which he sometimes claims merely to be eliciting, by questioning, the arguments of others and failing to reach a firm conclusion (see e.g. *Meno* 80c)).
ἐκβαλεῖν: 'to jettison', 'throw overboard'.

10(b8) τύχη: external events are 'accidents' in comparison with moral principles.
σχεδόν τι ὅμοιοι: 'pretty much the same (i.e. as before)...'

11(c1) πρεσβεύω: as transitive verb, is used chiefly in poetry of respect paid (e.g. to the gods), hence here gives an elevated tone: 'I revere...'

12(c2) ὧν: genitive of comparison; Literal tr. 'Than which if we can find nothing better to say...'

13(c3) οὐ μή...ξυγχωρήσω: οὐ μή + *aor. subj.* indicates emphasis.
ἄν: = ἐάν.

14(c3-4) πλείω: adverbial: 'even more than at present...' *or* accusative of respect: 'in respect to more things...'

15(c5) μορμολύττηται: Μορμώ was a bogey with which to frighten children. '...conjure up yet further goblins to frighten us with: chains etc.', humorous references back to C.'s warnings in Section IV.7-8(44e6).

16(c5) ἐπιπέμπουσα: almost mock heroic, often used of divine visitations: 'visiting upon us..'. The whole passage 14-16(c4-6) shows S. building up a humorous effect of mock-terror.

17(c7) πρῶτον μέν: this introduces S.'s initial position, the importance of the opinion of the expert over that of popular opinion, a frequent starting-point of Socrates, e.g. *La.*184d5; *Grg.* 460bff.(see Intro. section 3 (ii)).

18(c7-8) τὸν λόγον...ὃν σὺ λέγεις: C.'s reply to S. above at III.17-21(44d1-5).

19(d1) ἐλέγετο: for the force of the imperfect, see above n. on VI.9(b7). OCT²'s full-stop after δοξῶν (following Burnet) makes it clearer that the words following refer not to what C. said at III.17-21 (44d1-5 — he implied there that all opinions were important) but to Socrates' claims in 19-20(d1-2).

ἑκάστοτε: S. is presumably to be seen as referring C. back to various conversations he took part in as a friend of S. before the present crisis arose. The idea that all opinions are of equal significance is a possible implication of the fifth century sophist Protagoras (DK B1): πάντων χρημάτων μέτρον ἐστὶν ἄνθρωπος, τῶν μὲν ὄντων ὡς ἔστιν, τῶν δὲ οὐκ ὄντων ὡς οὐκ ἔστιν. ('Of all things the measure is man: of things that are, that they are; and of things that are not, that they are not'.).

20-23(d2-5) S. appears almost to be suggesting the view of Protagoras here in suggesting the relativity of views, not just between different individuals (see Prot. DK B1 above), but within the same individual at different times and in different circumstances.

22(d4) [ἕνεκα λόγου]: unlike Adam, most other texts (e.g. OCT²) do not bracket this phrase; it adds an important Platonic gloss on ἄλλως, in asking whether what S. (and, presumably, C.?) established before the present crisis arose was just spoken 'idly, for the sake of argument', or had real and permanent validity (for development of the idea of philosophy as not pertaining to real life, see esp. *Grg.* 485aff.).

24(d5-6) κοινῇ μετὰ σοῦ: *collaborative* investigation was a basic stated aim of the Platonic/Socratic dialectic, since it was essential that if there was to be unanimity about conclusions, intervening steps of the argument had to be agreed. S. is particularly keen to keep C. 'on board' in this instance, presumably in view of the gravity of the situation and C.'s strongly expressed contrary views. See esp. X.32(49d1)ff.

25(d6) ἀλλοιότερος: opposite of ὅμοιοι (10(b8) above). Up to this point, S. states, his conclusions seem not to have changed. It is now for C. and S.

to test further whether they are now in any way (τι) different (ἀλλοιότερος). The idea that arguments must always be subjected to continual investigation is a common belief of Plato's Socrates, (e.g. *Grg.* 481dff.). ὧδε: 'in this position' i.e. about to die. Contrast 27 (d8) below, where the meaning is 'thus'.

27(d8) τῶν οἰομένων τι λέγειν: see οἱ ἐπιεικέστατοι (n. on III.14(44c7) above). τι λέγειν: 'to say something (worth saying)'.

28(d9) νῦν δὴ: i.e. at 20(d1-2) above.

31-2(e3) ὅσα γε τἀνθρώπεια: 'in all human probability' (Tarrant).

32-3(e3-47a2) S.'s assumption that C.'s judgement will not be impaired because he doesn't have the prospect of death to lead his emotions astray is clearly a mild joke by S. at C.'s expense, in view of the contrast between C.'s and S.'s emotional state up to this point (see Adam, n. *ad loc* and Weiss, 43n.11).. Tarrant doesn't see the joke, but regards this as Plato's lapse, (n. *ad loc*).

34-7(a2-5) σκόπει δή: with these words S. initiates a brief 'question and answer' session with C., a characteristic form of Plato's style of argument in the Socratic dialogues, known as *dialectic.* The purpose of this particular exchange is to get C. to agree initially to what has up to now been merely asserted by S. — the distinction between informed and uninformed opinions. The repetition of this point might seem excessive, but C.'s sincere acceptance is vital for the subsequent attempt to undermine his initial position.

36(a4) after τὰς δ' οὔ, should be inserted words found in two MSS and read by Eusebius, <οὐδὲ πάντων ἀλλὰ τῶν μέν, τῶν δ'οὔ;>, included by OCT². Adam omits on the grounds that to mention distinction not only in opinions (some valid, some not) but also in people (the opinions of some persons are valid, of others not), anticipates the argument immediately below, 42-3(47a9-10). But anticipation is not to be ruled out.

39-40(a7) τὰς...χρηστὰς: 'good', with the implication of 'effective', 'serviceable', opposed to πονηρὰς = 'bad', 'worthless' 42(a9)ff. Note how, in equating the dichotomy of good/bad opinions with that of wise/foolish people (42-3), S., without actually arguing the point, is moving the emphasis away from the idea that an individual may have both good and bad opinions (a possible implication of 35-6 (a3-4) above) towards the idea of the expert, the wise person whose opinions will (all) be good.

Section VII. Socrates' reply: a review of basic Socratic principles (2), (47a12-47d7)

S. continues to outline a well-known Socratic position: when engaged in a particular activity one listens not indiscriminately, but to the expert in the field; but just as this is true in the case of e.g. physical training, the idea of expertise can also be extended to questions which are of present concern, i.e. issues concerning the just and the unjust etc.

1(47a12) τὰ τοιαῦτα ἐλέγετο: S. is here referring back to what are recognised as familiar Socratic examples of expertise which he was in the habit of (NB. imperfect ἐλέγετο) introducing, and which he now recalls for C.'s benefit (see e.g. *La.*184d).

5(b3) τυγχάνῃ...ὤν: '...who actually is (force of τυγχάνω here) his doctor or trainer'. For the coupling, in Plato, of the expertise of the doctor and trainer as both being concerned with the health of the body, see e.g. *Grg.* 452a6ff.

11(b8) δῆλα δή: 'Self-evidently', replies C, despite the fact that 9-10 (b6-7) blatantly contradicts what he asserted at III.17-18(44d1-2): ἀλλ' ὁρᾷς δὴ ὅτι ἀνάγκη, ὦ Σώκρατες, καὶ τῆς τῶν πολλῶν δόξης μέλειν. C. surely can't be that stupid! For the subordination of consistency of C.'s characterisation to the development of the argument, see Intro. section 2 (i).

12-15(b9-11) ταύτῃ...ἄλλοις: ταύτῃ goes closely with the verbal adjectives πρακτέον κτλ. Literal tr. 'One should act etc., then, in that way which seems good to him, the one man who is qualified etc...'. The verbal forms -εον occur with unusual frequency in *Crito*.
    ἐπιστάτῃ: 'overseer', 'instructor', often connected by Plato with ἐπίσταμαι, signifying 'one who knows', the 'expert' (see e.g. *Ap.* 20a8).

19(c2) λόγους: OCT² omits, understanding ἐπαίνους from the previous line.

23(c5-6) εἰς τί τῶν τοῦ ἀπειθοῦντος;: Lit.tr. '..with respect to which of the (parts) of the disobedient person?'

25(c8)ff. C. having agreed so far with S.'s examples, at this point S., under the guise of simply avoiding a long list (καὶ τἄλλα...ἵνα μὴ πάντα διίωμεν) uses the 'craft analogy' to move into what may seem to us like another area altogether, moral values, taking the, to us, highly questionable step that here also there is 'the man who understands' (ὁ ἐπαΐων), 'especially' (καὶ δὴ καὶ) with regard to issues related to good and bad, the just and unjust etc. Once again C. assents without demur (35(d7)).

27-8(c9-11) δίκαιων...κακῶν: note the arrangement of these polarised terms in AB-BA-AB order.

31(d2-3) αἰσχύνεσθαι καὶ φοβεῖσθαι: S. repeats key terms from C.'s παραίνεσις (Section IV.14(45a6), V.18(45e1), in order to emphasise that the same emotions now require a different, more worthy object.

μᾶλλον ἤ ξύμπαντας τοὺς ἄλλους: using a phrase repeated word-for-word from 14-15 (b11) above, where physical experts were being discussed, perhaps to smooth over a perceived 'bridge' between terms denoting technical expertise and those indicating moral value?

32-3(d4-5) ἐκεῖνο...ὃ...βέλτιον ἐγίγνετο: S. is referring, in a circumlocutory way, to the soul (ψυχή). The existence of some part of the individual which can be benefited/harmed by justice/injustice, just as the body can be benefited/harmed by good/bad physical influences, gives greater plausibility to the shift (as we might see it) in the argument from crafts to values. See further, Intro. section 3 (ii).

If S. is rehearsing arguments well-known to C. as a long-standing associate (N.B. ἐγίγνετο, imperfect, referring to past conversations on more than one occasion), the oblique reference to the soul would clinch C.'s assent (35(d7)).

Section VIII. Socrates' reply; a review of basic Socratic principles (3), (47d8-48b9).
The part of us which is impaired by unjust actions and benefited by just ones is more precious than the body; we therefore have that much more reason to pay attention to the expert on justice and injustice than to popular opinion. The power of the masses to inflict bodily harm on us does not affect the argument that the most important thing is to live well, that is, honourably and justly.

1(47d8) φέρε δή: S. marks the cumulative progress of the argument with such expressions, cf. εἶεν (VII.17(47c1)), φέρε δή (VII.1(a12)).

τὸ...βέλτιον γιγνόμενον...διαφθειρόμενον: ('the (part of us) becoming [better/worse])' is the object of διολέσωμεν. Literal tr.: 'If we destroy totally the (part of us) which becomes better through that which produces health but is destroyed by that causing disease...'

4-5(d10-e1) μή: note the position: Plato here wishes to emphasise the *failure to follow* expert opinion, and the corollary: ἀλλὰ τῇ τῶν πολλῶν can be understood.

ἆρα βιωτὸν...διεφθαρμένου αὐτοῦ;: Plato's S. uses this *ad hominem* argument elsewhere, e.g. *Grg.* 512a2ff. *Ad hominem* because, strictly speaking, for S., physical injury, illness etc. is not incompatible with living well, provided the soul is unaffected (see eg. *Ap.* 30a8-b1); but the point of the argument here as elsewhere, is to effect a comparison in value between body and soul (see below 17 (48a3)) by emphasising that, if a serious *bodily* ailment, e.g. an incurable disease, is popularly thought, eg. by C., to make life ἀβίωτος (see his answer at 10 (47e6)), how much less is life worth living if the *soul* is damaged.

6(e1-2) τὸ σῶμα: OCT² omits the definite article. σῶμα is the predicate: 'this (part) is surely [the] body.'

8-9(e4-5) See above on 4-5(d10-e1).

11-13(e7-8) Ἀλλὰ...ὀνίνησιν;: understand ἐστί with βιωτὸν, the phrase being postponed to give emphasis to ἐκείνου: 'But with *that* (part of us) destroyed...is life worth living for us?'

14(e9) ὅ τί ποτ᾽ ἐστί: why the 'intentional vagueness' (Burnet) in naming the part which good and evil benefit and harm? See also above VII.32-4(47d4-6). Possibly because the introduction of ψυχή would threaten to divert the argument into a metaphysical discussion which is not relevant to the urgently practical matter on which they are both engaged (on this point, see also Intro. section 3 (ii) and n.4).

τῶν ἡμετέρων: 'of our parts'. For a more extended discussion of the soul, see *Grg.* 477aff.

15(48a1) ἀδικία...ἡ δικαιοσύνη: S. starts to introduce the value terms on which C. based part of his Exhortation (IV.9(45a1); V.1(45c6)).

17(a3) τιμιώτερον: S. does not here produce the argument *why* the part with which justice and injustice are concerned is 'more to be valued' than the body. He is presented as running through positions with which C. can be presumed (however improbably in the context — see below on 25(48 a10)) to be familiar, and to be found elsewhere in the Socratic dialogues of Plato, eg., extensively, *Grg.* 464aff.

19-25(a5-10) This conclusion follows from S.'s previously stated (albeit here unargued) positions: *if* the expert in justice and injustice, and not the general public, has the power to affect the other 'more to be valued' part of us for good or ill, then on these subjects we ought to be concerned with the belief of the expert rather than 'the many', since that will be the truth.

23(a8-9) τῆς τῶν πολλῶν δόξης: genitive dependant on φροντίζειν.

25(a10) ἀλλὰ μὲν δή: adversative; 'But all the same...' (Tarrant). S. reintroduces C.'s second earlier point (above III.17-21(44d1-5)), as a hypothetical objection to the argument that only the expert has any claim on our attention. The objection that the power of physical compulsion must be weighed against that of the expert, and S.'s counter-demonstration that this apparent power is illusory, has its full exposition in the dialogue with Polus at Grg. 466bff. Here in Crito, as above (see n. on 17(a3) above), S. and C. are presented as merely asserting the conclusion of arguments mutually agreed in previous unspecified conversations.

26(a11) ἀποκτιννύναι: (OCT² ἀποκτεινύναι) preferred by Plato to ἀποκτείνειν (Adam).

27-9(b1-2) δῆλα δὴ καὶ ταῦτα...ὦ Σώκρατες. ΣΩ. Ἀληθῆ λέγεις: καὶ ταῦτα = 'this, too...', i.e. what has just been said, in addition to S.'s earlier point about the primacy of the expert. It is not clear what C.'s assent here signifies: is he merely uncontroversially *agreeing* with S. that it is 'clear' that public opinion 'would say that', or are we meant to detect an element of *support* for the actual position stated, i.e. it is 'clear' that the objection (that the many do have power) has weight (which would be consistent with his previous objection to S. at III.17(44d1)ff.), and that his coupling of this with S.'s previous points (i.e. 19-25(48a5-10) as 'clear' fails to discern that the two positions are, by implication, contradictory?

The apparent ambiguity in the significance of these words is compounded by a further uncertainty about the attribution of the words ἀληθῆ λέγεις. Burnet (OCT¹ and in his edition, n. *ad loc.*, following Schanz) takes ἀληθῆ λέγεις as still part of C.'s response and considers that Crito is supporting the actual sentiment (the many do have power): 'the threefold answer...suggests the eagerness of Crito to catch at any straw', obviously reading C. as affirming the substantial truth of what S. has just asserted (the many *do* have power), despite the contradiction with what he and S. have apparently just agreed (this interpretation is further strengthened with Schanz's suggested deletion of φαίη γὰρ ἄν in 27). The words could, however, even on this distribution between speakers, still support a less radical interpretation than Burnet's: C. is simply agreeing with S. that this is a popular view.

OCT², like Adam, gives the words ἀληθῆ λέγεις to S.; this distribution at least avoids ambiguity over whether C is or is not registering actual agreement with the sentiment in 25-6(a10-11); S. *cannot* be assenting to an approval by C. of the substantive position in 25-6 (that the many *do* have power) in which case we must assume, on this reading, that, as in the less radical interpretation of Burnet's distribution, in 27 C. is simply acknowledging that 25-6 is indeed what 'someone might say'.

Adam tries to have the dilemma both ways by suggesting, n. *ad loc.*, that 'δῆλα δή καὶ ταῦτα is an aside; the answer to Socrates' remark is contained in φαίη γὰρ ἄν', apparently assuming a C. who, whatever he may say openly to S., is not yet convinced of his reasoning; on this interpretation S.'s ἀληθῆ λέγεις presumably refers only to what he 'hears'. This seems an improbably complicated way to interpret the passage, with meagre dramatic warrant in the text.

A decisive answer is not possible; the OCT²/Adam distribution assumes (if we discount Adam's interpretation) that C. is simply affirming that 25-6(a10-11) is what 'people might say'. This then allows S. to agree in 29(b2). However, Burnet's more radical interpretation of his alternative (OCT¹) distribution can by no means be ruled out, and certainly not by the objection that, in assenting to the idea that the many have power, C. might thereby be contradicting himself. As we have seen, Plato presents C. as doing this elsewhere (see eg. VII.11 (47b8)).

29(b2) ὦ θαυμάσιε: ironic exclamation, which perhaps gives some support to the OCT¹ (Burnet) distribution of 27-9. S. is perhaps reacting to C.'s inconsistency: 'But, my dear man...'.

30(b2) τε: Michael Stokes (private communication) suggests γε here, giving a contrast between what has been agreed and what is to come: '*that* argument... still seems to me much as before...now look at this one too...'.

ὅμοιος...πρότερον: i.e. VII.1(47a12)ff.

31(b4) τόνδε: ie. a new point, as opposed to οὗτος (48b2)).

33(b5) τὸ εὖ ζῆν: once again, assertion of a position fully developed in *Grg.* 512d8ff. see also *Ap.* 28b 2ff.

34(b6) Ἀλλὰ μένει: ἀλλά here is strongly assentient (*GP* 20) 'But of course'. C.'s strong agreement is to be expected since 'living well' is self-evidently a desirable aim for all. But does C. really understand what S. means by the phrase?

35-7(b7-8) C.'s agreement to the equation of 'living well' with 'fine and just' living completes the final link in Socrates' argument:-

1. There are experts in good and evil analogous to experts in physical training, diet etc. These experts in good and evil are concerned with a part of us more precious than the body. Therefore, just as one will

benefit the body by obeying the advice of the expert in physical matters
and damage it by obeying popular (and so ignorant) opinion, so much
the more benefit/damage will result from obeying/disobeying the expert
concerned with the more precious part, which is concerned with good
(what is fine and just) and evil.
2. The most important thing in life is to live well.
3. Living well is to be equated with living finely and justly.
4. The conclusion is that whatever is just and fine (according to the expert)
should be done, since (combining 1 and 2 above) this will lead to living
well, which is the most important human aim.

**Section IX. Is or is it not just for S. to try to escape execution? (1),
(48b10-49a3)**
The only criterion to be considered is whether or not escape would be just.
Other considerations such as money and the raising of children are the
concerns of the ordinary public, who do not act according to reason.
Rather than continue to urge S. to escape without permission, C. should
try, if he can, to challenge S.'s arguments; then, and only then will S. listen
to him.

For the arguments of sections IX-X, see Intro. section 3 (ii).

1(48b10) ἐκ τῶν ὁμολογουμένων: ie. the two admissions VIII.31-
37(48b4-9) — steps 2. and 3. at the end of the previous section. Note that
it is vital for C. to have 'admitted' these points. This normal aspect of
Socrates' method, that the step-by-step development of the argument has
to be by mutual consent, so that S.'s interlocutor is finally compelled by
truth itself to concede the position reached, applies here even though S.
and C. are presented as merely recapping the conclusions of 'old'
arguments.

2(b10) σκεπτέον: see n. on VI.34-7(47a2-5).
    δίκαιον: S. prepares to challenge directly C.'s claim, at V.1(45c6)
above, that what he was doing was not δίκαιον.

3-4(b11-c1) μὴ ἀφιέντων Ἀθηναίων: 'the Athenians' here represent the
formal democratic government of the city as expressed through those
operating its legal institutions, in this case the popular jury. This is S.'s
first reference to a major aspect of his argument — whether 'the just' is
compatible with escape without official release.

6(c2-3) ἅς...τὰς σκέψεις: the relative clause precedes its antecedent in
order to put the emphasis on σύ. S. refers to what C. says in Sections IV
and V., and perhaps here, as elsewhere, fears that, despite his consistent

agreement in VI-VIII (46b1-48b9), C. has not abandoned his previous views.

8(c4) ταῦτα: subject of ᾗ, (referring back to σκέψεις) with σκέμματα as predicate. A word expressing fear or apprehension must be understood; tr.of 6-8: 'As to those considerations of yours on expenditure of money, reputation and raising of children, I fear that these are in truth the reflections...'

9-11(c5-6) See also above S.'s comment at III.22-27(44d6-10) on the masses doing, through ignorance, whatever 'they chance to do'. There is possibly an oblique reference to recent historical incidents during the Peloponnesian war in which the Athenian Assembly changed its mind after passing a capital sentence, eg. the illegal trial of the Athenian generals after the battle of Arginusae (406 BC), or, earlier, the change of heart in the debate over whether the inhabitants of Mytilene should receive severe punishment for defying the Athenians (Thuc. 3.36ff.; see also Intro. section 3 (iii) (2) and n.11). Such incidents might be unsympathetically described by Plato's S. as precipitated by those who 'lightly put to people death and would bring them back to life again, if they could...'

10-11(c6) τούτων τῶν πολλῶν: τούτων expressing contempt: 'these masses', pointedly contrasted with ἡμῖν δ' in the next sentence.

ὁ λόγος οὕτως αἱρεῖ: a basic Socratic principle — to follow the logic of the argument wherever it leads; for the phrase, see *R*.10.607b3.

12(c8) νῦν δὴ: ie. at IX.1(b10)ff. above.

15(d2) ἐξαγόμενοι: ie. S.'s friends ἐξαγόντες, and S. himself ἐξαγόμενοι(ος) (plural participle used loosely of S. after the plural subject). Will either group, rescuers or rescued, be acting justly?

τῇ ἀληθείᾳ: 'in truth'.

17-19(d4-6) ὑπολογίζεσθαι...παραμένοντας...πρὸ τοῦ ἀδικεῖν: strikingly similar in sentiment and wording to *Ap.* 28d8-10, where at his trial S. is justifying his refusal to abandon the philosophic life: ἐνταῦθα δεῖ, ὡς ἐμοὶ δοκεῖ, μένοντα κινδυνεύειν, μηδὲν ὑπολογιζόμενον μήτε θάνατον μήτε ἄλλο μηδὲν πρὸ τοῦ αἰσχροῦ. Such a sentiment might also at this point in *Crito* be thought to be leading naturally, as in *Apology*, towards a Socratic defence in terms of S.'s philosophic 'mission', mistakenly, as it turns out (see Intro. section 4 (ii)).

20-1(d7-8) Once again C. supports without protest — indeed enthusiastically — a conclusion which consigns his key arguments about money, reputation and childcare (sections III-V above) to oblivion.

Moreover he characteristically thinks that S.'s investigation is now over; that it is time simply to make a decision. S. immediately counters this in his next speech (σκοπῶμεν), with perhaps the slightest tinge of irony at C.'s naïve haste in ὦ ἀγαθέ.

26-7(e4-5) πεῖσαί σε...πράττειν: OCT² retains MSS order (which places ἀλλὰ μὴ ἄκοντος at the end of the sentence and changes πεῖσαί to πείσας. Adam's alterations are based partly on what he sees as the problems of ταῦτα πράττειν which, on the traditional reading, leave ταῦτα without a clear antecedent; Accordingly he takes πράττειν as co-ordinate with, and not subordinate to πεῖσαί; however the basic meaning is not seriously affected.

28-9(e5-49a1) τῆς σκέψεως...ἐρωτώμενον: a standard Socratic preamble to a dialectical argument; it is essential that C. does not answer contrary to his own convictions.

31(a3) ἀλλὰ: indicates consent (*GP* 16): 'Yes, well I will try'.

Section X. Is it, or is it not just for Socrates to try to escape execution? (2), (49a4-e8).
Do we still consider that we must never act unjustly or have our opinions changed with the circumstances? Surely it is still the case that it must be wrong to commit injustice irrespective of external circumstances. Further, we must not even return injustice for injustice because that is also to do an injustice. And doing an injustice is to wrong someone. Therefore one should never return injustice or wrong even in self-defence. C. must make sure he understands and agrees with this controversial position. Let us then take the argument a stage further: should one fulfil or renege on just agreements?

1(49a4) ἑκόντας ἀδικητέον εἶναι: not to act unjustly under any circumstances is a basic Socratic tenet (see eg. *Grg.* 469b8-9). S. also argues elsewhere that, strictly speaking, acting unjustly ἑκών ('willingly', 'knowingly', 'intentionally') is impossible, which is expressed in the Socratic tenet that 'virtue is knowledge' (knowing what is good entails doing it; wrongdoing must be the product of ignorance); see eg. *Ap.* 25d1ff.

4-5(a6-7) ἐν τῷ ἔμπροσθεν χρόνῳ: refers to previous conversations with C.; for Platonic exs. of this, see refs. in previous note.

7-8(a8-9) ἐκκεχυμέναι εἰσίν: ἐκχέω has a meaning v. similar to ἐκβάλλω (VI.9(46b7)); note the close repetition here of the ideas of VI.5-

26(46b4-d7). Repetition of ideas by S. is one of the particular characteristics of *Crito*, see eg. 37(d5)ff. below.

8(a9) ἄρα: expressing the surprise of disillusionment (*GP* 35), 'as it turns out'

τηλικοίδε: from *Ap.* 37d9 we learn that C. was about the same age as S., who was 70.

11(b1) παντὸς μᾶλλον: 'more than anything', ie. 'undoubtedly'.

14-15(b4-5) καὶ κακὸν καὶ αἰσχρὸν: note the combination of values here; S. wishes to deny totally the values of the conventional Athenian value system, which considers that the contrary, to *refrain* from returning injustice, is, in certain circumstances (ie. in self-defence) shameful (αἰσχρόν). For a more leisurely development of the argued case, see *Grg.* 474cff.

18(b8) Οὐ δῆτα: emphasis of 'expected denial' (*GP* 274). 'Certainly not'. It is, as we have already noted (see above n. on IX.20-1(48d7-8)), a weakness of characterisation of C. in *Crito* that he is presented at one time as 'having forgotten' and at others as emphatically endorsing Socratic doctrine.

22(c2) τί δὲ δή;: introducing a new point: 'So what about this then?'

κακουργεῖν: 'to do wrong', rather than 'inflict injuries' (Tarrant); see Intro. section 3 (ii).

23(c3) It could be argued that C.s strong denial here might be motivated by the form of the question: a prohibition against wronging another in isolation (eg. as a criminal action) might not seem so difficult to the conventional Crito (see Adam *ad loc.*). But this interpretation is not supported by 26(c6) below, where an equally emphatic denial greets S.'s question about the rightness of retaliation, which was fundamental to popular civic morality — ὡς οἱ πολλοί φασιν (23(c5)) (for a clear statement in Plato of the conventional position, see *Meno* 71e). For unconvincing attempts to reconcile Plato's S.'s position on this issue with that of Xenophon's S., see Adam, xviii n.1

27-9(c7-9) S. makes (and C. agrees to) a key move here: the equation of τὸ κακουργεῖν and τὸ ἀδικεῖν. C.'s emphatic agreement masks what could be challenged as controversial. According to the popular view τὸ κακουργεῖν and τὸ ἀδικεῖν might well not be equated; for example, it might well be δίκαιον to hurt somebody (not necessarily physically), eg. in retaliation for an injury inflicted ('reciprocity' was a traditional aspect of δίκη). But the common translation of δίκαιος/ἄδικος in a broad sense as 'right/wrong' tends to blur the distinction in English between the two words (see Intro. section 3 (ii) and n.5), and S.'s πού (27), presenting his equation of them as self-evident, may be what elicits the necessary endorsement from C.

30-31(c10-11) What follows these lines clearly underlines the weight they will be bearing in the subsequent argument. If the discussion is to proceed further, C. has to agree to the inadmissibility of committing an injustice (which is to be equated with doing wrong to someone — see above 27-9) in any circumstances whatever.

32(d1) καθομολογῶν: Adam points out (n. *ad loc.*) that the compound verb implies the piecemeal nature of agreement to the stages of S.'s. argument ('making these single admissions', Tarrant); while each step seems reasonable to the interlocutor, the final result may be indeed παρὰ δόξαν. Plato's S. also regularly reminds his interlocutors of the need for sincerity in answering his questions often as a prelude, or accompaniment to difficult or controversial arguments (see eg. *Grg.* 495a7-9ff). There may be a hidden irony here; in view of C.'s earlier παραίνεσις (sections III-V) there must be at least a suspicion on S.'s part that C. is replying παρὰ δόξαν (33), see nn. on VIII.27-9(48b1-2), IX.20-1(48d7-8), X.18(49b8). See further Weiss, 71).

36(d4) καταφρονεῖν: the dialectic of Plato's S. usually assumes at least the theoretical possibility of persuasion even in the case of antagonistic associates, eg. Kallikles (*Gorgias*) or Thrasymachos (*Republic* I); his statement here that there will be mutual contempt and (inevitably?) no κοινὴ βουλή (35(d3-4)) between those who accept his βουλεύματα and those who do not, may be an *ad hominem* device to underline for C. the importance of careful thought before acceptance.

37(d5) σκόπει δὴ οὖν καὶ σὺ εὖ μάλα: the build-up of emphasis here is a clear indication of the climax towards the central argument of the dialogue (see below Sections XI.ff.) with which C. has to be in agreement. This emphasis continues in the contrast κοινωνεῖς...ξυνδοκεῖ (37(d6)) with ἀφίστασαι...οὐ κοινωνεῖς (41-2(d9-e1)), and in the elaborate repetition (39(d7)ff.) of the main positions already established and agreed to by C. above at 16-29(b6-c9). Repetition of Socratic positions, rather than argument for them, seems typical of *Crito*. Here the somewhat earnest reiteration might further suggest S.'s unease at C.'s too ready agreement.

46(e4) ἀλλ᾽ ἐμμένω: ἀλλά turns S.'s conditional (εἰ δ᾽ ἐμμένεις: 44(e2-3)) into an emphatic statement of fact (*GP* 20). 'Indeed I do hold to it...so go on (ἀλλὰ), tell me'.

49(e6) δίκαια ὄντα: many things are unclear here: does 'if they are just' refer to the content of agreements or the terms on which they were made? And what does S. assume to be the content of such agreements? At this stage C. naturally agrees: the vague terms in which the question of 'keeping agreements' is put would make it hard for him (or any other Athenian) to do otherwise. Who would wish to advocate deception? But Crito does not yet realise to what this admission will lead (see Intro. section 3 (ii)).

This concludes the second of the three main divisions of *Crito*, which has been taken up with the brief rehearsal of Socratic beliefs essential as a basis for the subsequent argument. Having established the overriding importance of doing what is just and right, S. then builds on this base two propositions which assume great importance in the discourse of the Laws which follows:-
1. One should never do injustice or wrong (which amount to the same thing), even in retaliation for injustice.
2. One should fulfil just agreements.

Section XI. The Laws of Athens (1).The duty to obey so as not to destroy the Laws, (49e9-50c4).
If one ought to fulfil just agreements rather than break them, is an escape from prison not an injustice and so doing wrong to those least deserving of it? The Laws, if asked, would regard such an act as an attempt to destroy them, in that a city cannot continue to exist without legal judgements retaining their force. But can one not then reply that the city was itself guilty of an injustice against S, by virtue of a wrong judgement at his trial?

For the arguments of the remainder of the dialogue, see Intro. section 3 (iii) (1) 'The Laws' Case'.

1(49e9) ἐκ τούτων δή: thus S. marks the progressive nature of the argument; δή emphasises the importance of the positions just established: '[consider what follows] from these premises...' Cf. IX.1(48b10): ἐκ τῶν ὁμολογουμένων.

2(e9-50a1) μὴ πείσαντες: μή rather than οὐ to indicate that the participle is conditional: 'if we have not persuaded...'. For what has been thought to be the key role of persuasion in the argument with the Laws, see further, Intro. section 3 (iii) (2).

3(a1-2) καὶ ταῦτα: adverbial. Tr. '...and, into the bargain, those whom we least ought to wrong...'.

6-7(a4-5) C. has reached an *aporia* here, a stage characteristic of Plato's Socratic dialogues; he sees the step-by-step arguments he has agreed to (καθομολογῶν: X.32(49d1)) reaching unacceptable conclusions. Plato might also be using C.'s admitted puzzlement to signal the introduction of a difficult (because counter-intuitive) idea — a common Socratic ploy. For a different interpretation of the *aporia* see Intro. section 4 (iii).

9(a7) μέλλουσιν ἡμίν: dative dependant on ἐλθόντες... ἐπιστάντες.

ἀποδιδράσκειν : 'run away', 'flee', used of slaves, deserters. S. begins the argument with an already clear indication of how *he* views what C. euphemistically might call 'escape': ἀπιέναι, ἐξιέναι.

εἴθ' ὅπως...τοῦτο: added surely as an ironic side-swipe at C., rather than 'to spare Crito's feelings' (Adam).

10(a7-8) οἱ νόμοι καὶ τὸ κοινὸν τῆς πόλεως: speaking in the *persona* of somebody else, on his/her behalf, is an occasional device of Plato's Socrates (eg. *La.* 186d9ff. *Smp.* 201dff.)), but here despite the conditional ('*if* the Laws were to ask....') S. is presented as receiving the Laws almost as an external visitation (ἐπιστῆναι is regularly used of visions = 'appearing to...', from Homer onwards; see Burnet *n. ad loc.*). This sustained personification, unique in Plato, is given plausibility by the Greek idiom (again see Burnet) which allows the law to be a grammatical subject in such phrases as οἱ νόμοι οὐδὲν τούτῳ διαλέγονται 'The laws have nothing to say to him' ie. do not concern him (Demosthenes, *Against Makartatos* 59). The second phrase: τὸ κοινὸν τῆς πόλεως shows that Plato's S. intends 'the Laws' to be interpreted in the widest possible sense, as the embodiment of the legal, social and cultural authority of the *polis*. See Intro.section 4 (i).

13(b1) ἀπολέσαι: whether this 'destruction' which S. (hypothetically) contemplates could ever occur is debatable. It is clearly, in popular Athenian (or even our own) terms, counter-intuitive, but is made more plausible here by the personification: individual acts *can* 'destroy' people (as the Laws are here presented: ἡμᾶς: b1). The Laws seem to be suggesting that one violation contributes to the destruction of the whole system of law and even ξύμπασαν τὴν πόλιν τὸ σὸν μέρος.(14b2): 'as far as you are (personally) able', or maybe as a sarcastic aside 'as your contribution to the proceedings' (Campbell, *ad loc.*). For the 'consequentialist' argument — that S.'s contemplated act might in some way contribute to or actually cause the Laws' destruction — and an alternative interpretation, see Woozley, 111-29, and discussion in Intro. section 3 (iii) (2).

15(b3) ἀνατετράφθαι: 'be overturned', regularly used of the capsizing of a vessel, here metaphorically the 'ship of state'.

αἱ γενόμεναι δίκαι: ie., in this context, 'legal decisions made in court', specifically 'verdicts'.

16(b4) μηδὲν ἰσχύωσιν...ἄκυροι...διαφθείρονται: note the repeated, extreme language; the Laws' case is that S.'s act and others like it will destroy the whole system by rendering it ineffective. It is now possible to appreciate the importance S. attached to the 'ground-preparing' agreements between S. and C. above in Section X: *if* it can be established that by escaping S. would wrong the Laws, then, it has already been conceded, this would be an injustice towards them irrespective of the provocation offered (X. 24-29 (49c4-9)).

19(b7) ῥήτωρ: 'public speaker', 'advocate'. Burnet (and Adam) suggest a specific function has relevance here: a public advocate (σύνηγορος) appointed to defend laws which anyone was proposing to abrogate. The image is of the *rhetor* defending the Laws against S.'s 'proposal' (ie. the abolition of the law which requires legal judgements to be binding).

τούτου τοῦ νόμου ἀπολλυμένου...τὰς δίκας...κυρίας εἶναι: S. is envisaged as attempting to destroy (note again the strong language: ἀπολλυμένου) a law that decrees that judgements reached by a court shall be valid. This is the first aspect of the law which S.'s escape would potentially invalidate; he would not be abiding by the court verdict.

22(c1-2) ἠδίκει...ἡμᾶς ἡ πόλις: 'the *polis* was guilty...' the image is of the *polis* as defendant against the charge formally made by S.and C., that it had delivered a false verdict at S.'s trial. OCT² puts the phrase ἠδίκει...ἔκρινεν in quotation marks.

γὰρ...καὶ: γὰρ is explanatory here, the action explained being understood: '(Yes, we do contemplate this action) because the *polis* etc...'. καὶ is connective for causal: 'the *polis* is guilty *because* it did not...'

24(c4) C. naturally seizes on S.'s explanation as the obvious pretext for disobedience: the court's verdict in S.'s case was unjust. Is it not, therefore, strange that this pretext did not explicitly feature in his Exhortation above (see Section V summary and Intro. section 3 (i))?

Section XII. The Laws of Athens (2). The duty to obey as son to parent, (50c5-51c5)

The Laws question whether that (ie. only to obey when the verdict is considered just) was the agreement made between them and S. On the contrary, since it was under their auspices he was given life, nurtured and educated, he does not, any more than a slave with respect to his master, have rights equal to those of the Laws. Indeed, the city commands even greater respect than that which should be given to parents. You must either persuade your country of its error, or do whatever it orders in war or the lawcourts or anywhere else.

2(c6) καὶ ταῦτα ὡμολόγητο ἡμῖν καὶ σοί: 'this too..', ie. the dispensation not to obey an unjust verdict (XI.21-3(c1-3)).

Plato is introducing here the idea of law as a contract between the state and the citizen, though at this stage of the dialogue it is not yet clear what was the nature of the 'agreement' between the Laws and S., and how it was made.

δίκαις: see above on XI.15(b3).

4-5(c7) θαυμάζοιμεν: in suggesting S.'s and C.'s surprise, Plato is also reflecting a probable audience reaction to a new and possibly controversial idea.

7-8(c9-10) ἀποκρίνου...ἐρωτᾶν...ἀποκρίνεσθαι: Plato's regular way of describing the Socratic method, see eg. *La.* 187c1ff., *Prt.* 336c4., *Phd.* 75d2.

9(c10) τί ἐγκαλῶν;: a rhetorical question in that S. has already specified the charge above (XI.22-3(c1-2)). The Laws are simply implying that that particular charge will not stick, for the reasons they are about to give. Alternatively (see Weiss, 94) τί might be read absolutely, making the question genuine: 'Why, charging us and the city [ref to 22-3 (c1-2) above], are you attempting to destroy us?'

10(d1) ἀπολλύναι: see above on XI.13(b1).

σε ἐγεννήσαμεν: the Laws 'brought forth' S. in the sense explained in 11-12: they sanctioned the legal union of his parents under which he was born. In Athens legitimate birth was a vital aspect of citizenship, since it was the basis of all citizen rights, especially those concerning succession to property.

13-14(d4) τοῖς νόμοις τοῖς περὶ τοὺς γάμους: laws which established the legal validity of marriage and hence the legitimacy of children.

14(d5) οὐ μέμφομαι; S. is here presenting himself in a role which is normally taken by his interlocutors — that of the compliant 'feed' (see also below 19(e1)).

15(d6) τροφήν καὶ παιδείαν: ie. the basic upbringing of the child. S. (for purposes of the argument?) is here presented as uncritical of conventional Athenian education, contrary to his view in eg. *Laches, Apology* and, especially, *Gorgias.* The charge that Socrates encouraged children not to respect their parents can be found in Xen. *Mem.* I.2.49, and Xen. *Ap.* 20, and may have been a popular view of him, reflected in Aristophanes, *Clouds* (see below n. on 29 (51a1-2)). S.'s more critical view of Athenian education according to Plato might be better represented in *Prt.* 339ff., where Plato has S. caricature the conventional interpretation of traditional Greek poetry.

ἡμῶν: taken with οἱ...νόμοι: 'those of us Laws assigned to these matters...'

17(d8) παραγγέλλοντες: we know of no Athenian laws which compelled parents to educate their sons, though Solon the sixth century statesman and legislator had laid down in detail what 'free children' should learn. S.'s point here has rhetorical effectiveness: παραγγέλλω can have overtones of 'recommend, exhort' (weaker than κελεύω: LSJ).

18(d8-e1) μουσικῇ καὶ γυμναστικῇ: the standard Athenian education. 'Music' covered the whole literary side of standard education, 'gymnastic' the physical side.

21(e3-4) ἔκγονος καὶ δοῦλος: from what has preceded S. might be seen, metaphorically speaking, as the laws' offspring, but how can he be seen as their 'slave'? The idea of the law as the (only) 'master' curtailing individual license is however common in Athenian rhetoric of the fifth and fourth centuries BC, emphasising the qualities of the Greek *polis* as opposed to non-Greek subjection to individuals; see eg. Hdt.7.104, Plato, *R.* 563d; *Laws,* 700a. The Laws' argument here owes more to borrowed ideology than logic.

23(e5) ἆρ᾽ ἐξ ἴσου...τὸ δίκαιον: This is a second strand to the argument; retaliation (ie. escape) should not be attempted because it is defying a higher authority. τὸ δίκαιον is not ἐξ ἴσου between the Laws and S., any more than it is between father and son, or between master and slave. The force of the prohibition derives, it seems, from the operation of the analogy; yet the metaphor of the Laws 'parenthood' is required to bear an excessive argumentative weight in this passage. (see below note on 25-35 (e7-51a7)).

25(e7) ἀντιποιεῖν: S. and C. have already agreed that this is unjust in any circumstances at X.19-29 (49b9-c9); in strict logic the present argument is therefore superfluous. But see further Intro. section 3 (iii) (1).

25-35(e7-51a7) πρὸς μὲν ἄρα (25(e7))...καὶ πρὸς (26(e8))... πρὸς δὲ...ἄρα (30(51a2-3)): note the strong rhetorical binding of this long sentence leading to the climax of 30: is it the case that you may not retaliate in these 'unequal' situations (parent/child, master/slave) while this will be permitted to you in the case of the Laws, who are, by implication, the supreme parent or master (and note the enhancement of the Laws' status by the introduction of τὴν πατρίδα with τοὺς νόμους)? Plato seems here to be using rhetoric to bolster up the rather questionable logic of the analogy between parent and Laws.

29(a1-2) τυπτόμενον ἀντιτύπτειν: this recalls the comic reversal in Aristophanes *Clouds*, where Pheidippides tries to justify beating his father Strepsiades (1321ff.). The Laws' analogy gains force from the Athenian context in which there were strong legal sanctions against, and also popular moral disapproval of, maltreatment of parents (κάκωσις γονέων); one of the questions asked of a candidate for public office at the *dokimasia* (scrutiny of fitness for office) was whether he treated his parents well ([Aristotle], *Ath.* 55.3-4).

30(a3) ἔσται: OCT² with most editors reads MSS ἐξέσται and places a comma after σοι.

34-5(a7) ὁ...ἐπιμελόμενος: sarcastic, since devotion to ἀρετή was a cornerstone of S.'s 'mission' (see eg. *Ap.* 30a-b); the reference here also recalls C.'s reproach to S. at V.16-17(45d8-9). As Adam remarks, n. *ad loc.*, 'ἐπιμελεῖσθαι indeed was almost a technical term in Socrates' preaching'. The tone is continued in σοφός which frequently has a pejorative connotation in Plato, eg. *Ap.* 18b7.

35-51(a7-c3) ἢ οὕτως...ὅτι κτλ.: This second of the two long rhetorically constructed sentences has the effect of reinforcing the importance of the relationship οὐκ ἐξ ἴσου between S. and the Laws, by ranging over the social areas of the *polis* in which almost unquestioning obedience is required. The persuasive power of the sentence is more dependent on patriotic rhetoric than on logic: note especially:-
1. the substitution of ἡ πατρίς for οἱ νόμοι in the latter part of the sentence, both with ἡ πόλις (48-9(b10)) and on its own (37(a9), 41(b2-3), 51(c3)), which suggests that the Laws are sliding the argument towards a patriotic, and away from a strictly socio-legal emphasis (nb. the word-play πατρίδα/πατέρα (41(b3-4)), and, specifically to strengthen the analogy, 50-1(c2-3); the 'father/mother — native land' analogy is reintroduced at the end). And note the nature of words used to describe it: 37-8(a9-b1): τιμιώτερον...σεμνότερον...ἁγιώτερον. 39-40 (b1-2): καὶ παρὰ θεοῖς καὶ παρ' ἀνθρώποις...σέβεσθαι. The description of respect due to the Laws takes on an almost theological tone here.

2. Repetition of tricola ('three limbed' phrases — a stock rhetorical device) in 'crescendo' to reinforce the build-up: 43-4 (b5-6) ἐάν τε τύπτεσθαι ἐάν τε δεῖσθαι, ἐάν τε εἰς πόλεμον ἄγῃ. 46-7 (b8-9) καὶ οὐχὶ ὑπεικτέον οὐδὲ ἀναχωρητέον οὐδὲ λειπτέον τὴν τάξιν. 47-8 (b9-10) ἀλλὰ καὶ ἐν πολέμῳ καὶ ἐν δικαστηρίῳ καὶ πανταχοῦ ποιητέον.

3. The careful placing of the telling polarity πείθειν...βιάζεσθαι (49-50 (c1)): Πειθώ/Βία (persuasion/force) play a major part in Athenian images of their superiority to other Greeks in the value they placed on persuasion over force (Isocrates, *Antidosis*, 294). Once again, the ideological emphasis (see above on 25-35 (50e7-51a7)) enables the Laws to disguise their own authoritarian stance by presenting themselves as open to persuasion. See R. G. Buxton, *Persuasion in Greek Tragedy: a Study of Peitho*, Cambridge, 1982, 58-63.

4. The close link between legal and military compulsion (47-8 (b9-10): καὶ ἐν πολέμῳ καὶ ἐν δικαστηρίῳ...ποιητέον). This conjunction may have seemed less strange to a fifth/fourth century audience than to us, since the deliberative guise of the *polis* (eg. deciding on war and peace) and its legal role were more closely allied than in a modern context. Even so, however, Plato here allows Socrates to slide over obvious differences between obeying military orders on campaign and obeying the decision of a court. Moreover it is significant that in the *Apology* S. uses the military/legal analogy to justify *defiance* of the court: at *Ap.* 28e-29a he presents the analogy of not deserting his military assignments (with strikingly similar language to *Crito*: 29a1: λίποιμι τὴν τάξιν/*Cri.* 46-7 (51b9) λειπτέον τὴν τάξιν), to justify 'staying at his post', ie. continue to conduct philosophical investigations even if this should be forbidden by the court (*Ap.* 29c6-d1) (though Socrates may perhaps be presenting only a hypothetical case, see Intro. section 4 (i)). In *Crito* such behaviour is presented as an example of the lengths to which the *obedient* citizen should go to in order to satisfy the Laws' demands.

41-2(b4) ἢ πείθειν ἢ ποιεῖν ἃ ἂν κελεύῃ: 'persuade or obey'; the citizen could 'persuade' the Laws, for example, by convincing a jury of his innocence while defending a law-suit; the persuasion must be successful, however, if it is to be an alternative to obedience; the emphasis in some interpretations on the opportunities the citizen has to persuade (see notably Kraut 55-90) is not borne out by the language used to describe the individual's relationship with the laws: σέβεσθαι = 'reverence', 'worship'; (40(b2)) ὑπείκειν = 'yield to' (b3); θωπεύειν = 'flatter', 'wheedle'. See further Intro. section 3 (iii) (2).

Section XIII. The Laws of Athens (3). The duty to obey by virtue of having chosen to stay in Athens, (51c6-52a3) The Laws have reared S. and given him a good environment in which to live. On the other hand, he has always been free to leave the city if he wishes, without loss of property. By staying he is implicitly agreeing either to persuade or obey.

1(51c6) σκόπει τοίνυν: (cf.XI.8(50a6), ἀλλ᾽ ὧδε σκόπει). This is a new stage in the argument: the Laws are stating that, by escaping, S. would not be acting justly. Strictly speaking, they have attempted to argue this already (previous section); but the 'argument from agreement' seems to be logically distinct from the 'parent/child' analogy. See following note and Intro. section 3 (iii).

5(c8-9) γεννήσαντες, ἐκθρέψαντες, παιδεύσαντες: cf. above XII.10 (50d1)ff. But the earlier argument implied compulsion (S. as the ἔκγονος καὶ δοῦλος: 50e3-4); here, as we shall see, it hinges on agreement. Are the Laws preparing to shift their ground here?

6-7(c9-d1) Plato here tries to weld the logically distinct conceptions (see previous note) together by drawing on the conception of Athenian laws in the broadest sense as providing a total cultural environment for their citizens, and not just legal injunctions and prohibitions; cf. Pericles' Funeral Speech, esp. Thuc. 2.40ff.

8-9(d1-2) προαγορεύομεν τῷ ἐξουσίαν πεποιηκέναι Ἀθηναίων τῷ βουλομένῳ: 'we publicly proclaim, by having given permission to any Athenian who wishes...'.The infinitive dependant on ἐξουσίαν (ἐξεῖναι) has to wait until 11 (d5). The awkwardness of the syntax suggests a formal and solemn legal pronouncement: προαγορεύω = 'proclaim (by herald)'; τῷ βουλομένῳ suggests the phrase indicating a request for speakers in the Assembly: τίς ἀγορεύειν βούλεται; (Aristophanes, *Acharnians*, 45).

9(d3) δοκιμασθῇ: this refers to the *dokimasia* 'scrutiny', by the *Boule* (Council), of youths of 18 about to be confirmed in citizenship by being enrolled in the register of their deme, at which point they became *epheboi* (see above n. on XII.29 (51a1-2) for *dokimasia* on entry to public office). The Laws see this as being the obvious time for the newly adult citizen to 'renew' the 'contract'. See Kraut, 154.

11(d5) ἀπιέναι: the first introduction in the Laws' speech of the theme of exile which plays an increasingly important role in the remainder of the dialogue.

14-15(d7-8) ἀποικίαν...μετοικεῖν: distinguishes an Athenian 'colony' (ἀποικία) from emigration (μετοικεῖν) out of the area of Athenian influence. Note the emphasis on keeping property in voluntary exile, as opposed to a severe legal penalty which might involve forfeiture of property.

17(e2) παραμείνῃ: stronger than 'stay', = 'stand one's ground' (Tarrant).

17-18(e2-3) τάς τε δίκας δικάζομεν καὶ τἄλλα τὴν πόλιν διοικοῦμεν: the first phrase refers to the administration of justice, but in the second the close link with all other aspects of the *polis* as it affects the individual is emphasised. Two important unargued assumptions underpin the Laws' case in this section:-

1. 'The way we organise the city in other ways' (18(e3)), is so closely related to 'the way we administer justice' (17-18(e2-3)), that a refusal to obey the latter is in effect a refusal to accept the organisation of the whole *polis*.
2. The Laws represent an indivisible whole: a refusal to obey one allegedly faulty verdict is in effect an attack not only on the whole legal system, but on the *polis* in general.

19(e4) ὡμολογηκέναι ἔργῳ ἡμῖν: this is the crux of the Laws' position: they argue that simply by not leaving Athens a citizen has *explicitly* (ἔργῳ) entered into a contract with the city to 'persuade or obey' (22-3).

21-2(e6) γεννηταῖς οὖσιν ἡμῖν...τροφεῦσι: the Laws make further use of the 'parent' analogy (see above XII.10(50d1)ff.). The 'tricolon crescendo' structure of 20-27(e5-52a3), with the main point in the much-extended third member (22-7), repeats the highly rhetorical tone of Section XII above.

22-3(e7) πείθεσθαι: OCT² has future infinitive πείσεσθαι, which makes more sense: 'having agreed that he would obey us...'.

24(52a1) καὶ οὐκ ἀγρίως ἐπιταττόντων: the point the Laws wish to make here is that they are not tyrants arbitrarily imposing their will. Citizens are allowed the chance of persuasion in due legal process; yet, once this process has been duly completed, dissent is not acceptable (see above on XII.41-2 (51b4)).

Section XIV. The Laws of Athens (4). Socrates' own record as an 'obedient' citizen, (52a3-53a8)
On these terms, S. would be one of the most guilty if he were to escape, because he more than most has shown himself satisfied with the city: he

has hardly ever left it, he has fathered children in it, and at his trial did not propose banishment as an alternative punishment, but claimed that he would prefer death. But now he is trying to escape. Are we, the Laws, right about S.'s agreement with us, or not?

1(52a3) Σώκρατες: Adam following Schanz, omits the usual ὦ before S.'s name (following one MS) arguing increased impressiveness; it is hard to see why here particularly. Most editors (Burnet, OCT²) include it.

καὶ σέ: 'you too', as well as the hypothetical Athenian of the previous section (8-9).

8(a8) ὁμολογίαν: 'compact', 'agreement': to follow and respect the dictates of the *polis* in return for participation in ἁπάντων...καλῶν (XIII.6-7 (51c9-d1)). Because of his alleged reluctance to travel abroad, S. is supposed to be particularly enthusiastic about this compact, as the language indicates: ἐγὼ...ὡμολογηκὼς τυγχάνω...'*I* actually had made this agreement more emphatically...'.

10(b2) ἡμεῖς...καὶ ἡ πόλις: here closely associated, but not it seems identified (see below, 18(c1)), where the Laws refer to 'we and our *polis*'). A central feature of the Laws' argument, as we have seen above (Section XII), is the vagueness of the relationship (often with strong implications of identity) between οἱ νόμοι, ἡ πόλις and ἡ πατρίς.

14(b6) [ὅτι μὴ ἅπαξ εἰς Ἰσθμόν]: Adam omits these words, which are included by Burnet and OCT² after ἐξῆλθες. The MSS evidence is inconclusive, and mention of the journey 'to the Isthmus' (of Corinth — for the games, presumably) does not occur elsewhere in Plato; but the words were read by Athenaeus (216b.), and Plato (*Phaedrus* 230c-d) does not really contradict them (Phaedrus jokingly says that S. never sets foot outside the city, but the observation is very general and is expressed in the present tense).

ποι στρατευσόμενος: see *Ap.* 28e. and *La.* 181a-b. for S.'s military service.

19(c2) πολιτεύσεσθαι: to be interpreted in a minimal sense: 'living in the *polis* as a citizen' (see also below 33(d5)); Plato's S. presents himself as having deliberately steered clear of active politics (*Ap.* 31cff.). See Intro. section 4 (i).

20(c2-3) καὶ παῖδας...ἐποιήσω: a somewhat strained point; S. is hardly exceptional in having fathered children at Athens, and this has a rather loose connection with his supposed contentment with the city (20-1(c3)).

21(c4) ἔτι τοίνυν: introducing a further item in a series; 'And, again...' (*GP* 576).

ἐν αὐτῇ τῇ δίκῃ: Plato presents S. (ie. the Laws) as referring to his refusal at his recent trial, according to Plato, *Ap.* 37b-38b., to propose the penalty of exile which there was every reason to suppose the jury would have accepted (τῆς πόλεως...τότε ἑκούσης 23(c5-6)) instead of death. In an ἀγὼν τιμητός, a suit where there was no fixed penalty, as was the case in the charge of impiety against S., it would have been prudent of him to propose a penalty which the jury might at least regard as realistically severe. According to Plato *Apology*, S. (ultimately) proposed a reasonable penalty, a fine of 30 minae, but the jury reacted by voting for death. In *Apology*, refusal to take the option of exile is closely bound up with S.'s 'mission'. But here in *Crito* the Laws take this failure to propose the alternative penalty of exile as yet further evidence of S.'s general satisfaction with the institutions of Athens. Burnet is misled by this intertextuality (see also above, IV.25(45b7)), into claiming this passage as 'testimony to the historical truth of the *Apology*' (n. on 52 c7). All it does demonstrate, however, is the partial correspondence on this point between the two dialogues of Plato. For yet another interpretation of S.'s attitude to the prospect of death, see Xen. *Ap.* 23. See Intro. section 1.

24(c6) ἐκαλλωπίζου: possibly an allusion to *Ap.* 37c-38a; yet producing κεκαλλιεπημένους...λόγους is just what at the beginning of his defence speech S. says he is *not* planning to do (*Ap.* 17b9).

27-8(c9-d1) ἐπιχειρῶν διαφθεῖραι: for this idea, see above, section XI.13 (50b1).

29(d2) ἀποδιδράσκειν: 'to run away' (of a slave); see above n. on XI.9 (50a7).

τὰς ξυνθήκας τε καὶ τὰς ὁμολογίας: duplicating and making plural S.'s 'agreement' is perhaps intended to conceal vagueness (see also below, 37-8 (d9-e1). What is it (are they)? When is he supposed to have made it (them)? Why are the Laws not more precise here?

33(d6) ἔργῳ, ἀλλ᾽ οὐ λόγῳ: the Laws concede here the absence of a verbal compact, but clearly intend the 'agreement in deed' to indicate stronger commitment on S.'s part than a verbal agreement would have given. Yet, as Tarrant remarks (n. *ad loc.*), in this particular instance it is the *absence* of a verbal aspect to the compact which might seem to weaken their case (on this see Weiss, 114n.69, though she misrepresents Adam as joining some editors in incorrectly understanding the ἀλλ᾽ οὐ λόγῳ phrase as 'not in *mere* words'). For a detailed philosophical discussion of the contractual issue, especially on the question of implicit agreement, see Woozley, 76ff.

38(d9-e1) πρὸς ἡμᾶς αὐτούς: 'with us in person' (Burnet).

38-40(e1-3) παραβαίνεις, οὐχ ὑπὸ ἀνάγκης...οὐδε ἀπατηθεὶς οὐδὲ ἐν ὀλίγῳ χρόνῳ ἀναγκασθείς: this is presented as a legal image: παραβαίνεις is the technical term for transgressing a law, eg. breach of contract (συνθήκης παραβάσεως δίκη); against which it was possible to plead deception, duress and time-pressure. In S.'s 'contract' with the Laws, they claim that none of these can be represented as invalidating the agreement.

41(e3-4) ἐν ἔτεσιν ἑβδομήκοντα: a rhetorical exaggeration; S. could only be envisaged as having had the time from eg. his *dokimasia* to make an informed decision.

43-4(e5-6) οὔτε Λακεδαίμονα...οὔτε Κρήτην: Socrates is presented by Xenophon as strongly approving of Spartan obedience to the law (*Mem.* IV.4.15). See also *R.*, VIII. 544c (Adam also quotes Plato, *Prt.* 342aff., but this is in a joking context). S. and his followers had a popular reputation as 'Laconian', see Aristophanes *Birds* 1281-3 (and see n. *ad loc.* in N. Dunbar, Aristophanes, *Birds*, Oxford, 1995).

45-6(53a2) βαρβαρικῶν: OCT² reads βαρβάρων.

47-9(a3-5) οὕτω σοι διαφερόντως...ἤρεσκεν ἡ πόλις καὶ ἡμεῖς οἱ νόμοι: largely literal repetition of 10-13 (52b2-5) above marks the boundaries of this particular motif.

49(a5) γὰρ: explains the addition in the previous phrase (καὶ ἡμεῖς οἱ νόμοι) and why this addition should be obvious; '(your satisfaction with us the laws as well) for who...?'

50((a6) νῦν δὲ δὴ: emphatic; 'And now, after all this...' (Tarrant).

51-2(a6-7) ἐὰν ἡμῖν γε πείθῃ: this reference to persuasion marks the end of this section of the argument, cf. C.'s παραίνεσις, IV.11 (45a4), V.33 (46a8-9).

γε...γε: 'Yes, (you will), if you take our advice...then at least you will not be a laughing-stock...'

Section XV. The Laws of Athens (5). The disadvantages, for Socrates, of escape, (53a9-54b2).
If S. were to escape, his friends might well suffer legal penalties as a consequence. And S. himself would not be welcome, as a destroyer of laws, in well-governed cities. Furthermore, even if he were to go to such places, would he have the nerve to repeat his large claims for goodness and justice, and so confirm our verdict on him? On the other hand, if he were to go to C.'s friends in Thessaly, he would be a source of amusing stories — a laughing-stock. And would he be any better able to look after his children if he were in Thessaly than his friends could if he were dead?

1(53a9) Σκόπει γὰρ δή: the combination of particles arrests attention (*GP* 243), with γὰρ implying a link in argument with the previous section: 'For just consider now...'; the mode of address recalls XI.8 (50a6) and XIII.1 (51c6).

ταῦτα: ie. the 'contract(s)' between the citizen and the Laws. Again (see n. on XIV.29(52d2)) plurality seems to cover vagueness.

ἐξαμαρτάνων: note present participle, as opposed to the single act of aorist παραβὰς. The escape is also of course a formal infringement of the law.

2(a9-10) τούτων: ref. to the (unspecified) plurality of agreements.

4-7(b1-3) A direct answer to C. who. made light of these possibilities in section IV. 2-9 (44e2-6) above, and even suggested (14(45a6)ff.) that money would fix the συκοφάνται through whose actions S.'s helpers might be in danger of prosecution.

5(b1-2) καὶ αὐτοί: ie. as well as you.

7(b3) αὐτὸς δὲ πρῶτον μὲν: αὐτὸς δὲ answers ὅτι μὲν γὰρ above at 4(b1). πρῶτον μὲν, the first of S.'s alternative moves, has to wait until 25(d1) below for the second alternative: ἥξεις δὲ εἰς Θετταλίαν...;

9(b5) εὐνομοῦνται γὰρ ἀμφότεραι: both Thebes and Megara were oligarchies at this time, and S. had friends in both *poleis* (for Thebes, see above, IV.22-3 (45b4-5)). The Laws' point here is that S.'s action at Athens in 'destroying' the laws will be seen as a threat to a city with good laws (literal meaning of εὔνομος). The 'well-governed' cities are in contrast with 24 (d1)ff. below. But could either of these cities (Thebes or Megara) be described as having the kinds of institution which would even in the first place allow the 'contract' which S. might break?

10(b5) πολέμιος: 'an enemy of the state'.

12-16(b7-c3) The charge against S. is outlined at *Ap.* 24b8-c1. Both aspects, destroying the laws and corrupting the youth of Athens, appear to have been current accusations, and, as here, they were clearly linked: see Xen. *Mem.* I.1.49-50, I.2.9. Only the latter appears to have been part of the official indictment (see Intro. section 1). The rare word for 'destroyer', διαφθορεὺς, here (12(b7)) and repeated at 14-15 (c1), might possibly be echoing the anti-Socrates speech of Polykrates in the 390's BC. See further, Intro. section 4 (ii).

15-16(c2-3) σφόδρα που δόξειεν ἄν...εἶναι: the ironically assumed diffidence of που here with σφόδρα emphasises the speaker's certainty that the latter misdemeanour follows from the former: 'For whoever is a destroyer of laws is very likely, one supposes, to be seen as a destroyer of young and foolish people'.

It is significant that, while S.'s (i.e. the Laws') criticisms of himself refer, within the dramatic structure of *Crito*, only to the injustice of escape (which, of course, is only hypothetical because it is not going to happen), Plato appears to be broadening the canvas here to include the general criticisms of S. found elsewhere, eg. in Xenophon and Polykrates, and implying that if S. had escaped, such judgements on Socrates would indeed have been vindicated.

21-2(c7-9) ἡ ἀρετὴ καὶ δικαιοσύνη...καὶ τὰ νόμιμα καὶ οἱ νόμοι: this is an interesting representation of S.'s teaching: Plato's dialogues give us clear evidence of S.'s concern for the former, but the latter is not easy to find, and the most celebrated reference to the former (*Ap.* 30a-b) does not include the latter. Is the separation of the two groups of subjects in the sentence, with the second placed almost as an afterthought (22), a sign of Plato's unease with two different representations of S., or possibly intended as a retrospective justification of S. aimed at his more conservative supporters? See Intro. section 4 (ii).

23(c9) ἄσχημον: 'unseemly', 'discreditable', because rendering his teaching hypocritical through his betrayal, in practice, of his principles. But, surely, this would be so only if he included the latter group (above 22) among his teachings. Adherence to the former would not necessarily be inconsistent with S.'s escape. But the Laws clearly intend ἀρετή and δικαιοσύνη to be inseparable from adherence to the *nomoi*, and this, of course, begs *the* chief interpretative question of *Crito* — the significance of the Laws' speech.

τὸ τοῦ Σωκράτους πρᾶγμα: for an element of contempt in this expression, see Adam, n. *ad loc.*

24(d1) οἴεσθαί γε χρή: γε sharpens the command here (*GP* 125). 'You certainly ought to think so!'.

26-7(d3) πλείστη ἀταξία καὶ ἀκολασία: a standard assumption among Athenians, stated as self-evident by the Laws (γὰρ δὴ: 'without a doubt') when describing a district with a non-constitutional government (see Xen. *Mem.* I.2.24). Thessaly had only recently emerged from a primitive form of government noted for the striving for political domination of various aristocratic families, and the late fifth/early fourth century was marked by short-lived tyranny and general civil strife. S. is not very sensitive to C.'s feelings, considering the latter's links with the state, see IV.28-31 (45c2-5).

28-30(d5-7) ἀπεδίδρασκες...ἀποδιδράσκοντες: ἀπεδίδρασκες might be seen as a 'pictorial imperfect' (Adam) — heightening the ridiculous by allowing us actually to picture the scene of S. fleeing in disguise. The fullest presentation of the 'escaped slave' motif as a representation of the nature of S.'s flight; see above, XI.9 (50a7), XIV.29 (52d1-2).

29d6) οἷα δὴ: 'The note of disparagement, irony or contempt is rarely quite absent' (*GP* 220). 'the kind of get-up...'

31(d8)ff. See *Ap.* 37cff. for S.'s views on the indignity of clinging to life at any price.

33(e1) αἰσχρῶς: Burnet and OCT² take the alternative, and more convincing MS reading γλίσχρως = 'greedily'. For the MS. confusion, see Burnet, *ad loc.*

34(e2) οὐδεὶς ὅς ἐρεῖ;: main clause governing ὅτι κτλ. (31 (d8)ff.), postponed for rhetorical effect.

37(e5) εὐωχούμενος ἐν Θετταλίᾳ: a proverbial expression for wild self-indulgence: 'roistering in Thessaly'; see Aristophanes, *Frogs*, 85.

39(54a1) περὶ δικαιοσύνης τε καὶ τῆς ἄλλης ἀρετῆς: these discussions of Plato's S. form the major part of the Socratic dialogues. The only extant dialogue, however, which deals directly with δικαιοσύνη as its chief subject is *Republic.*

40(a2) ἀλλὰ δὴ: introducing a counter-argument 'But you will answer that...' This particular argument is exactly that of C. at V.6-14 (45c10-d6): that in staying in Athens for execution S. would be deserting his children.

43(a4-5) ξένους...ἀπολαύσωσιν;: heavily ironic: the children will be foreigners in Thessaly, having also been deprived of Athenian citizenship along with their father.

45(a7) μὴ ξυνόντος σοῦ αὐτοῖς: '...seeing that you won't be there for them'; ie. they would be just as well off in his absence from Athens as if he were dead. Tarrant (211n.56) on no textual warrant inserts<καὶ> before μὴ, and his translation 'even without you there' misses the point: will S.'s still being alive affect the upbringing of his sons for the better, *seeing that* he will be absent. Tredennick's minimalist tr. 'without you', (Penguin 1st ed.) at least avoids the wrong emphasis.

46(a7) γὰρ: suggests an answer to the previous question: '(Yes, it will), for your friends etc...'.

47-9(a8-10) ἐὰν...ἐὰν δὲ: exact repetition of words, with play on ἀποδημήσῃς ('migrate to Thessaly' or 'to Hades'). For the idea of death as 'migration' see *Ap.* 40e4-5: εἰ δ' αὖ οἷον ἀποδημῆσαί ἐστιν ὁ θάνατος ἐνθένδε εἰς ἄλλον τόπον....

50(b1-2) Exact repetition in the last three words of 24 (53d1) above rounds off this portion of the argument.

Section XVI The Laws of Athens (6). The Laws summarise their argument and predict S.'s unfavourable reception in Hades if he ignores their advice, (54b3-d2)
Nothing is more important than doing what is just, especially when S. comes to plead his case in the next world. He will go there as a victim of a wrong decision made not by the Laws but by his fellow citizens. But if he injures the Laws in return for their injury he will face the Laws of Hades in the next world. He should take the Laws' advice in preference to C.'s.

1(54b3) Ἀλλ': see above III.1 (44b3).

2(b3) τοῖς σοῖς τροφεῦσι: see above XIII.5 (51c8-9).

5-6(b6) τοῖς ἐκεῖ ἄρχουσιν: S. here begins to reintroduce the religious, prophetic tone found in the dream introduced at the start of the dialogue (II.14-20 (44a10-b5)). Traditionally there are three judges of the Underworld, Minos, Rhadamanthys and Aiakos, who had the reputation of having been just men in their lifetime and received their status in the Underworld as a reward. The introduction of the theme of the afterlife into ethical discourse is a feature of the conclusion of several of Plato's dialogues and takes its tone from the nature of what precedes it. For

example, in *Ap.* 41a a discursive meditation on what awaits the condemned
S. after death reinforces his belief that there is nothing to be feared by him;
in *Grg.*523aff. and *R.*614bff., on the other hand, eschatological myths
elaborate on the fate of the individual soul after death which serve as a
religious confirmation of the dialectical argument.

6-7(54b7-8) δικαιότερον...ὁσιώτερον: the spheres of humans and gods
respectively.

The allusions here add emphasis to the Laws' argument by picturing
the (unnamed) judges as more weighty versions of their brothers above
(see below 16 (c6-7)). The equation of personal, albeit semi-divine judges
in Hades with the personified abstraction of 'the Laws' nevertheless
fudges precisely the tricky issue underlying Plato's argument: how far are
the Laws to be equated with actual judges, individually or collectively (see
further below on 10-11 (c1-2))?

9(b9) νῦν μ ν: 'as it is'.

10-11(c1-2) ἠδικημένος...οὐχ ὑφ' ἡμῶν τῶν νόμων ἀλλά ὑπὸ
ἀνθρώπων: one of the few occasions on which the Laws actually admit
that there has been a miscarriage of justice (see also above XI.21-3 (50c1-
3) for S.'s assertion of the injustice). But can the Laws actually avoid
implication in injustice done to S. by an Athenian jury in their name? A
crucial problem with the Laws' argument in *Crito* is that Plato appears to
want to allow them to have it both ways: the Laws can, as on this occasion,
distance themselves from the individual mistakes of their fallible
representatives, i.e. Athenian juries, while at the same time relying on the
argument that allegiance to them (the Laws) entails obedience to the unjust
decisions of those representatives. See further on this, Intro. section 4 (i) &
(ii).

11-12(c2-3) ἀνταδικήσας τε καὶ ἀντικακουργήσας: Adam's comment
(n. *ad loc.*) that these words 'have for their object not the laws, but the
δικασταί' begs precisely the question raised in the previous note.

14-15(c5-6) σαυτόν τε καὶ φίλους καὶ πατρίδα καὶ ἡμᾶς: this
rhetorical conflation of distinct groups avoids analysis of precisely the
problems noted above in 10-11.

16-17(c6-7) οἱ ἡμέτεροι ἀδελφοὶ οἱ ἐν "Αιδου νόμοι: do the Laws
identify the νόμοι of the Underworld with τοῖς ἐκεῖ ἄρχουσιν (see 5-6
above and n.)? The conflation of personal and abstract (crucial, as we have
seen above (10), to the Laws' argument) would not seem strange to S.'s
contemporaries, being used to the personification of, eg. Δίκη, see e.g.

Antigone's reference (Soph. *Ant.* 451) to ἡ ξύνοικος τῶν κάτω θεῶν Δίκη.

18(d1) τὸ σὸν μέρος: as at XI.14 (50b2) above; the Laws seem to feel the counter-intuitive absurdity of implying that S. single-handedly can 'destroy' (ἀπολέσαι) them.

ἀλλὰ: the word indicates a slight break before the Laws' final appeal to S.: 'Come now,...' (*GP* 15).

19(d1) ἃ λέγει: i.e. sections III-V.

Section XVII. S.'s Peroration, (54d3-e2).

Following his extended representation of the Laws, S. returns to his own *persona* to liken the force of what he has 'heard' to the sound of ritualistic music ringing in his ears, against which it will be useless to argue. C. is asked if he has anything further to say; he declines, and S. confirms that he will follow his intended course.

1(54d3) ὦ φίλε ἑταῖρε Κρίτων: Adam (n *ad loc.*) notes the pathos of this unusually long mode of address, surely in a sense valedictory for C. personally.

2-3(d4-5) ὥσπερ οἱ κορυβαντιῶντες τῶν αὐλῶν δοκοῦσιν ἀκούειν: the Korybantes were originally priests of the Phrygian goddess Kybele, (a cult introduced into Athens in the late fifth century), who performed frenzied dancing to flutes and drums. S.'s points are that the sound continues to reverberate in his ears after it has finished *and* that it drowns out all other sounds. S.'s reversion to quasi-religious imagery matches his recounting of the dream at the beginning of the dialogue (section II). Although formally a simile (S. says that his reception of the Laws' words is 'like' (ὥσπερ) a mystic trance), the addition of emphasis: αὕτη ἡ ἠχὴ τούτων τῶν λόγων ('it is *this* sound of *these* words'), with the image maintained in βομβεῖ, seems to be suggesting that the sound of the Laws' words is so powerful as to drown out other sounds, rendering him incapable of listening to other arguments (rather like the effect of a tinnitus — Campbell n. *ad loc.*). Adam suggests that the sound and effect of the Laws' discourse is intended to resemble S.'s 'divine sign' (*Ap.* 40aff.), but S.'s description here suggests something much more insistent.

2-6(d3-6) δοκῶ ἀκούειν...δοκοῦσιν ἀκούειν...τῶν ἄλλων ἀκούειν: earlier editors preferred excision to avoid the repetition of ἀκούειν (see Cobet, quoted in Burnet, n. *ad loc.*). But quite apart from this kind of exact repetition being a general stylistic feature of *Crito*, surely this particular repetition may be deliberately intended to illustrate the continual and repeated ringing in S.'s ears of the 'korybantic' Laws' arguments.

6-7(d6-7) ὅσα γε τὰ νῦν ἐμοὶ δοκοῦντα: an element of caution integral to the provisional and progressive nature of Plato's Socratic dialectic (see *Grg.* 527a, *R.* 506e). It sits rather oddly in the context of convinced assertion produced by the Laws. And S. is likely to be dead before much further progression is possible!

7-8(d8) ὅμως...λέγε: S. maintains the collaborative illusion until the very end. But C. has long since ceased to argue.

10(e2) ταύτῃ: ie. the path the Laws propose: to accept the death penalty.

11(e2) ὁ θεὸς ὑφηγεῖται: the singular θεὸς recalls the end of *Ap.*(42a5), but also represents the final conflation of authority figures which underpin the overwhelming force (if not logical consistency) of the argument — Laws (νόμοι), city (πόλις), native land (πατρίς) and, finally, god (ὁ θεὸς).

Bibliography

Editions and translations

Adam, J., *Plato,* Crito (ed.), (2nd ed. Cambridge, 1891, repr., Bristol, 1988).

Burnet, J., *Platonis Opera* I (Oxford Classical Text) (Oxford, 1900).

Burnet, J., *Plato*: Euthyphro, Apology and Crito, *edited with notes* (1st ed. 1924, repr. Oxford, 1954).

Campbell, M., (ed.), *Plato,* Crito, *with commentary and vocabulary (A Greek Prose Reading Course for Post-Beginners, Unit 2: Philosophy)*, (Bristol, 1997).

Croiset, M., *Crito* in *Platon, Oeuvres Complètes* I (Paris, 2nd. ed. 1953).

Duke, E.A., Hicken, W.F., Nicholl, W.S.M., Robinson, D.B., Strachan, J.C.G., *Platonis Opera* I, (Oxford Classical Text, new ed., containing *Crito*, ed. Nicholl) (Oxford, 1995).

Fowler, H.N., *Plato* I: *Euthyphro, Apology, Crito, etc.*, (Loeb ed., Cambridge Mass. and London, 1914).

Tarrant, H., *Plato: The Last Days of Socrates, rev. of tr. by H. Tredennick, with new Introduction and Notes*, (London, 1993).

Warrington, J., *The Trial and Death of Socrates: Euthyphro, Apology, Crito, etc. tr. with an Introduction*, (London, 1963).

Watt, A.F., *Plato,* Crito, ed., (London, 1927).

West, T.G., and West, G.S., *Plato and Aristophanes: Four Texts on Socrates* (Ithaca, N.Y., 1984).

General

Adkins, A.W.H., *Merit and Responsibility*, (Oxford, 1960).

Allen, R.E., *Socrates and Legal Obligation*, (Minneapolis, 1980).

Bostock, D., 'The Interpretation of Plato's *Crito*', Phronesis 35 (1990), 1-20.

Brickhouse, T.C. and Smith, N.D., (1) *Socrates on Trial*, (Oxford, 1989).

Brickhouse, T.C. and Smith, N.D., (2) *Plato's Socrates*, (New York/Oxford, 1994)

Brown, H. 'The structure of Plato's *Crito.*' Apeiron 25 (1992), 67-82.

Carter, L.B., *The Quiet Athenian*, (Oxford, 1986).

Clay, D., 'The origins of the Socratic dialogue.' in P.A. Vander Waerdt (ed.), *The Socratic Movement*, (Ithaca/London, 1994), 23-47.

94

Colson, D.D., (1) 'On appealing to Athenian law to justify Socrates' disobedience', Apeiron 19 (1985), 133-51.

Colson, D.D., (2) 'Crito 51A-C: to what does Socrates owe obedience?', Phronesis, 34 (1989), 27-55.

DeFilippo, J.G., 'Justice and obedience in the Crito', Ancient Philosophy 11 (1991), 249-63.

Dover, K.J., Greek Popular Morality in the Time of Plato and Aristotle, (Oxford, 1974).

Ferguson, J., Socrates: A Source Book, (London, 1970).

Gronewald, M., 'Sokratischer Dialog', Kölner Papyri, 5 (1985), 33-53.

Irwin, T., 'Socratic Enquiry and Politics', Ethics 96 (1986), 400-15

Kahn, C.H., 'Did Plato write Socratic dialogues?' Classical Quarterly 31 (1981), 305-20.

Kraut, R., Socrates and the State, (Princeton, 1984).

Ledger, G.R., Recounting Plato: a Computer Analysis of Plato's Style, (Oxford, 1989).

MacDowell, D.M., The Law in Classical Athens, (London, 1978).

Miller, M., '"The arguments I seem to hear": argument and irony in Crito', Phronesis 41 (1996), 121-37.

Ostwald, M., Nomos and the Beginnings of the Athenian Democracy, (Oxford, 1969).

Penner, T., 'Two notes on the Crito: the impotence of the many, and "Persuade or Obey"', Classical Quarterly, 47 (1997), 153-66.

Santas, G., Socrates: Philosophy in Plato's Early Dialogues, (London, 1979).

Saunders, T.J., Plato: Early Socratic Dialogues, (London, 1987).

Stephens, J., 'Socrates on the rule of law', History of Philosophy Quarterly 2 (1985), 3-10.

Stokes, M.C., (1) Plato's Socratic Conversations, (London, 1986).

Stokes, M.C., (2) Plato: Apology of Socrates, edited with an Introduction, Translation and Commentary, (Warminster, 1997).

Thesleff, H., 'Platonic Chronology', Phronesis 34 (1989), 1-26.

Vlastos, G., (1) 'Socrates on political obedience and disobedience', Yale Review 63 (1974), 517-34.

Vlastos, G., (2) Socrates: Ironist and Moral Philosopher, (Ithaca, 1991).

Weiss, R., Socrates Dissatisfied: an Analysis of Plato's Crito, (New York/Oxford, 1998).

White, J.B., 'Plato's Crito: the authority of law and philosophy', in R.B. Louden and P. Schollmeier, The Greeks and Us: Essays in Honour of Arthur W.H.Adkins, (Chicago, 1996), 97-144.

Woozley, R.D., Law and Obedience: the Argument of Plato's Crito, (London, 1979).

Vocabulary

ABBREVIATIONS

acc.	accusative	num.	numeral
adj.	adjective	opt.	optative
adv.	adverb	part.	participle
aor.	aorist	partic.	particle
comp.	comparative	pass.	passive
conj.	conjunction	perf.	perfect
dat.	dative	pers.	person
dem.	demonstrative	pl.	plural
fut.	future	plup.	pluperfect
gen.	genitive	possess.	possessive
imperat.	imperative.	prep.	preposition
impers.	impersonal	pres.	present
ind.	indicative	pron.	pronoun
indef.	indefinite	reflex.	reflexive
inf.	infinitive	rel.	relative
interrog.	interrogative	sing.	singular
mid.	middle voice.	subj.	subjunctive
n.f.	noun, feminine	superl.	superlative
n.m.	noun, masculine	v.	verb
n.n.	noun, neuter		

A

ἀγαθός: adj., good
ἀγανακτέω: v., be angry, displeased
ἀγαπάω: v., love
ἀγγελία: n.f., message, news
ἄγγελος: n.m., messenger
ἅγιος: adj., holy
ἀγρίως: adv., wildly
ἀγρυπνία: n.f., sleeplessness
ἄγω: v., lead, bring (ἡσυχίαν ἄγειν: be at ease)

ἀγών: n.m., trial, struggle
ἀδελφός: n.m., brother
ἀδικέω: v., wrong, do injustice
ἀδικία: n.f., wrong, injustice
ἄδικος: adj., wrong, unjust
ἀδύνατος: adj., unable, impossible
ἀεί: adv., always, ever
Ἀθηναῖος: adj., Athenian
ἀθρέω: v., look closely at, consider
Ἅιδης: n.m., Hades

αίρέω: v., take, seize, prove; mid. choose, prefer

αἰσθάνομαι: v., perceive, feel, understand

αἰσχίων: adj., comp. of αἰσχρός, baser, more disgraceful

αἰσχύνομαι: v., be ashamed

αἰτία: n.f., blame, charge, cause

ἀκολασία: n.f., intemperance, licentiousness

ἀκολουθέω: v., follow

ἀκούω: v., hear, listen to

ἄκυρος: adj., without authority

ἄκων: adj., unwilling

ἀλήθεια: n.f., truth

ἀληθής: adj., true

ἀληθῶς: adv., truly, actually

ἁλίσκομαι: v. pass., to be caught, taken

ἀλλά: conj., but

ἄλλῃ: adv., elsewhere, in another way

ἀλλήλους (ἀλλήλων, ἀλλήλοις): pron., each other

ἀλλοῖος: adj., different

ἄλλος: adj., another, other

ἄλλοσε: adv., to another place

ἄλλοτε: adv., at another time

ἄλλως: adv., otherwise, at random; (ἄλλως τε καὶ, especially)

ἅμα: adv., at the same time

ἀμείνων: adj., (comp. ἀγαθός) better

ἀμελέω: v., neglect, have no care for

ἀμύνω: v., ward off, (mid.) defend oneself

ἀμφότερος: adj., each of two, (pl.) both

ἀναβιώσκομαι: v., bring back to life

ἀναγκάζω: v., compel

ἀνάγκη: n.f., necessity, compulsion

ἀναισχυντέω: v., be shameless

ἀναλαμβάνω: v., take up, resume

ἀναλίσκω: v., spend, use up

ἀνάλωσις: n.f., expenditure

ἀνανδρία: n.f., cowardice

ἀνάξιος: adj., unworthy

ἀνάπηρος: adj., maimed

ἀνατρέπω: v., overturn

ἀναχωρέω: v., retreat

ἀνδρεῖος: adj., brave

ἄνευ: prep. (+gen.) without

ἀνήρ: n.m., man

ἀνθρώπειος: adj., human

ἄνθρωπος: n.m., human being

ἀνόητος: adj., foolish, unreasonable

ἀνταδικέω: v., return injustice

ἀνταπόλλυμι: v., destroy in return

ἀντιδράω: v., do in return, retaliate

ἀντικακουργέω: v., to wrong in return

ἀντιλέγω: v., speak in reply, speak against

ἀντιποιέω: v., do in return

ἀντιτύπτω: v., beat in return

ἄξιος: adj., worthy

ἀπαγγέλλω: v., bring news, report

ἀπαγορεύω: v., forbid, dissuade

ἀπαίρω: v., carry away, depart

ἅπας: adj., all, everyone

ἀπατάω: v., cheat, deceive

ἀπειθέω: v., be disobedient

ἄπειμι (inf. -ἰέναι): v., go away

ἄπειμι (inf. -εῖναι): v., be absent

ἀπέρχομαι: v., go away, depart from

ἀπό: prep., (+gen.) from, away from

ἀποβάλλω: v., throw away, reject
ἀποδημέω: v., be away from home, go abroad
ἀποδημία: n.f., being away from home, residence abroad
ἀποδιδράσκω: v., run away
ἀποθνήσκω: v., die
ἀποικία: n.f., colony
ἀποκάμνω: v., grow quite weary, cease to, shrink from doing
ἀποκρίνομαι: v., answer, reply
ἀποκτίννυμι: v., kill
ἀπολαύω: v., enjoy, profit from
ἀπόλλυμι: v., destroy utterly, (mid.) perish
ἀπολογέομαι: v., defend oneself
ἆρα: partic., used to introduce a question
ἄρα: partic., so, then, accordingly
ἀργύριον: n.n., silver, money
ἀρέσκω: v., please
ἀρετή: n.f., goodness, excellence
ἄρτι: adv., just now, recently
ἀρχή: n.f., beginning, rule, government
ἄρχω: v., rule, (mid.) begin
ἀσπάζομαι: v., greet, welcome
ἀσφάλεια: n.f., safety, security
ἀσχήμων: adj., unseemly
ἀταξία: n.f., disorder, lack of discipline
ἀτιμάζω: v., dishonour
ἄτοπος: adj., extraordinary, strange
ἄττα = τινά: (see τις)
ἄττα = ἄτινα: (see ὅστις)
αὖ: adv., again
αὐλός: n.m., flute
αὔριον: adv., tomorrow
αὐτόν (see ἑαυτόν)
αὐτός: pron., self, himself (ὁ αὐτός: the same)
αὐτοῦ: adv. here

ἀφαίρεσις: n.f., taking away, confiscation
ἀφίημι: v., let go, give up, permit
ἀφικνέομαι: v., arrive at, reach, come to
ἀφίστημι: v., put away, remove, (pass.) withdraw
ἄφρων: adj., foolish

B

βαθύς: adj., deep
βαρβαρικός: adj., barbarian
βαρύς: adj., heavy, grievous
βεβαιόω: v., make firm, establish
βέλτιστος: adj., (superl. ἀγαθός), best
βελτίων: adj., (comp. ἀγαθός), better
βιάζω: v., force, constrain
βίος: n.m., life
βιόω: v., live
βιωτός: adj., worth living for, to be lived
βομβέω: v., hum, buzz
βούλευμα: n.n, plan, resolution
βουλεύω: v., consider, take counsel, (pass.) be resolved
βουλή: n.f., will, counsel, plan
βούλομαι: v., wish, want

Γ

γάμος: n.m., marriage
γάρ: partic., for
γε: partic., at least, at any rate
γελοίως: adv., absurdly
γεννάω: v., beget, bring forth
γεννήτης: n.m., parent
γέρων: n.m., old man
γίγνομαι: v., become, happen, be born
γυμνάζω: v., train, exercise, practise

γυμναστικός: *adj.*, of gymnastics, (γυμναστική τέχνη = art of gymnastics)
γυνή: *n.f.*, woman

Δ

δαιμόνιος: *adj.*, miraculous, marvellous; used in vocative: ὦ δαιμόνιε, my good sir
δεῖ: *v.impers.*, it is necessary
δεῖπνον: *n.n.*, food, meal
δεσμός: *n.m.*, bond, fetter
δεσμωτήριον: *n.n*, prison
δεσπότης: *n.m.*, master, owner
δεῦρο: *adv.*, hither
δέω: *v.*, bind
δή: *partic.*, indeed (for emphasis)
δῆλος: *adj.*, clear, obvious
Δῆλος: *n.f.*, Delos
δήπου: *partic.*, doubtless, I presume
δῆτα: *partic.* certainly, surely (emphatic form of δή)
διά: *prep.*, (+*acc*) because of, (+*gen.*) through, by means of
Δία: *acc.* of Ζευς
διαβάλλω: *v.* slander, misrepresent
διάγω: *v.*, pass time, pass one's life
διαλέγομαι: *v.*, converse, discuss
διάλογος: *n.m.*, conversation, dialogue
διανοέομαι: *v.*, have in mind, intend
διαφερόντως: *adv.*, differently from, above all others
διαφέρω: *v.*, differ from
διαφεύγω: *v.*, escape, get away from
διαφθείρω: *v.*, destroy, kill, corrupt
διαφθορεύς: *n.m.*, destroyer

διδάσκω: *v.*, teach
δίειμι: *v.*, go through, discuss
διέρχομαι: *v.*, go through, narrate
δικάζω: *v.*, give judgement
δίκαιος: *adj.*, just, right
δικαιοσύνη: *n.f.*, justice, righteousness
δικαστήριον: *n.n.*, court of justice
δικαστής: *n.m.*, judge, juror
δίκη: *n.f.*, justice, decision, lawsuit, penalty
διοικέω: *v.*, control, administer (the state)
διόλλυμι: *v.*, destroy utterly
διφθέρα: *n.f.*, leather garment
δοκέω: *v.*, seem (δοκεῖ μοι *impers.* it seems to me, I think)
δοκιμάζω: *v.*, approve, sanction, (*pass.*) be admitted to the rights of adulthood
δόξα: *n.f.*, opinion, reputation
δοξάζω: *v.*, hold an opinion, judge
δουλεύω: *v.*, be a slave to, serve
δοῦλος: *n.m.*, slave
δράω: *v.*, do, accomplish
δύναμαι: *v.*, be able
δύναμις: *n.f.*, strength, power, ability
δυνατός: *adj.*, powerful, able, possible
δύω: *num.*, two
δυσχερής: *adj.*, hard to manage, annoying

Ε

ἐάν: *conj.*, if
ἑαυτόν: *reflex. pron.*, himself
ἐάω: *v.*, allow, concede, permit
ἑβδομήκοντα: *num.*, seventy
ἐγγύς: *adv.*, near, *pron.* (+*gen.*) near
ἐγείρω: *v.*, rouse, awaken

ἐγκαλέω: ν., accuse, indict, charge with

ἐγώ: pron., I (ἔγωγε, emphatic)

ἐδεστέον: verbal adj., one must eat

ἐθέλω: ν., wish, be willing, want

ἔθος: n.n., custom, habit

εἰ: conj., if

εἰδέναι: ν., inf., οἶδα

εἰδώς: part., οἶδα

εἶεν: interjection., well!

εἰκός: n. part. ἔοικα

εἰμί: ν., be

εἶμι: ν., will go

εἷς: num. one

εἰς: prep. (+acc.) into, to

εἰσέρχομαι: ν., go into, enter

εἰσηγέομαι: ν., introduce, bring forward, explain

εἴσοδος: n.f., entry

εἶτα: adv., then, next

εἴτε...εἴτε: conj., either...or

εἴωθα: ν., be accustomed

ἐκ: prep. (+gen.), out of, from

ἑκάστοτε: adv., on each occasion

ἐκβάλλω: ν., throw out, throw aside

ἔκγονος: adj., descended from, (n.) child

ἐκεῖ: adv., there

ἐκεῖνος: pron., that (person etc.)

ἐκεῖσε: adv., thither

ἐκκλέπτω: ν., steal, carry off

ἐκπαιδεύω: ν., bring up from a child, train thoroughly

ἐκτός: adv., prep.(+ gen.) without, outside of,

ἐκτρέφω: ν., rear, bring up from childhood

ἐκχέω: ν., pour out, squander

ἑκών: adj., willing

ἐλάττων: (comp. μικρός), less

Ἑλληνίς: adj. f., Greek

ἐμμένω: ν., abide by, hold to (a belief)

ἐμός: possess. adj., my, mine

ἐμποδών: adv., in the way

ἔμπροσθεν: adv., before

ἐν: prep.(+dat.), in

ἐναντίος: adj., opposite, contrary

ἐναργής: adj., clear, bright, distinct

ἕνεκα: prep. (+gen.) on account of

ἐνέχω: ν., hold fast, (pass.) be held by, be entangled in

ἐνθάδε: adv., here

ἐνθένδε: adv., hence, from the following

ἐννοέω: ν., reflect on, consider, understand

ἐνσκευάζω: ν., get ready, prepare, (mid.) dress oneself up

ἐντεῦθεν: adv., from there, thereupon

ἐντρέπω: ν., turn about, (mid.) respect, reverence

ἐνύπνιον: n.n., dream

ἐξάγω: ν., lead out, bring out

ἐξαμαρτάνω: ν., err greatly, mistake entirely

ἐξαπατάω: ν., deceive, deceive thoroughly

ἔξειμι: ν., go out

ἐξεργάζομαι: ν., work out, bring to perfection

ἐξέρχομαι: ν., come out

ἔξεστι: ν. impers., it is possible

ἐξουσία: n.f., power, authority

ἔοικα: ν., (perf. with pres. sense) seem, am likely

ἔπαινος: n.m., approval, commendation

ἐπαΐω: ν., hear, understand

ἐπεγείρω: ν., awaken

ἐπεί: conj., when, since

ἐπειδή: *conj.*, since, after that
ἔπειμι: *v.*, go to, approach
ἔπειτα: *conj.*, then, next
ἐπί: *prep.*, (*+acc.*) towards,
  against, (*+gen.*) on upon,
  (*+dat.*) at, over, for
ἐπιδημέω: *v.*, live at home
ἐπιεικής: *adj.*, fitting, reasonable
ἐπιθυμέω: *v.*, desire, long for
ἐπιθυμία: *n.f.*, desire, longing
ἐπιλύω: *v.*, loose, release, *mid.*
  afford relief from
ἐπιμέλομαι: *v.*, care for, cultivate
ἐπινοέω: *v.*, think on, contrive
ἐπιπέμπω: *v.*, send after, send
  against
ἐπισκοπέω: *v.*, look upon,
  examine
ἐπιστάτης: *n.m.*, master, lord
ἐπιτάττω: *v.*, set in command,
  order
ἐπιτήδειος: *adj.*, suitable, fit,
  (*n.m.*) close friend
ἐπιτηδές: *adv.*, on purpose,
  advisedly
ἐπιχειρέω: *v.*, attempt, undertake
ἕπομαι: *v.*, follow
ἐργάζομαι: *v.*, work, make,
  accomplish, be busy
ἔργον: *n.n*, work, deed
ἐρίβωλος: *adj.*, very fertile
ἔρχομαι: *v.*, come, go
ἐρῶ: *v.*, will say (*serving as future
  of* φημί)
ἐρωτάω: *v.*, ask
ἑταῖρος: *n.m.*, companion,
  comrade
ἕτερος: *adj.*, the other, one of two
ἔτι: *adv.*, further, yet, still
ἑτοῖμος: *adj.*, ready, prepared
ἔτος: *n.n.*, year
εὖ: *adv.*, well
εὐδαιμονίζω: *v.*, call happy

εὐειδής: *adj.*, well shaped,
  beautiful
εὐεργετέω: *v.*, do a kindness to
εὐθύς: *adv.*, straight, immediately
εὐμενῶς: *adv.*, kindly, graciously
εὐνομέομαι: *v.*, have good laws
εὑρίσκω: *v.*, find
εὐτελής: *adj.*, cheap
εὐωχέω: *v.*, entertain hospitably,
  (*pass.*) feast sumptuously
ἐφίημι: *v.*, let go, permit
ἐφίστημι: *v.*, set *or* place upon,
  (*2nd aor. & perf. act.*) stand
  upon
ἐχθρός: *adj.*, hostile, (*n.m.*)
  enemy
ἔχω: *v.*, have, hold

Z
ζάω: *v.*, live
Ζεύς: *n.m.*, Zeus

Η
ἤ: *partic.*, *indicates a question*
ἤ: *conj.*, or, than,
ἡγέομαι: *v.*, lead, think, consider
ἤδη: *adv.*, now, already
ἡδύς: *adj.*, sweet, pleasant
  (ἡδέως: *adv.*, sweetly, gladly)
ἥκιστα: *superl. adv.*, least
ἥκω: *v.*, have come
ἡλικία: *n.f.*, age, time of life
ἦμαρ: *n.n*, day
ἡμεῖς: *pers. pron.*, we
ἡμέρα: *n.f.*, day
ἡμέτερος: *possess.adj.*, our
ἡσυχία: *n.f.*, rest, quiet
ἥττων: *comp. adj.*, less
ἤχη: *n.f.*, sound

Θ
θάνατος: *n.m.*, death

101

θάτερον: (= τὸ ἕτερον), see
ἕτερος
θαυμάζω: v., admire, wonder at
θαυμάσιος:, adj., wonderful,
admirable
θέλω = ἐθέλω
θεός: n.m., god
Θετταλία: n.f., Thessaly
θεωρία: n.f., viewing, spectating
Θηβαῖος: adj., Theban
θνήσκω: v., die
θωπεύω: v., flatter, cajole

I
ἰατρός: n.m., doctor
ἰδιώτης: n.m., private person
ἱκανός: adj., sufficient, adequate
ἱκνέομαι: v., come, arrive
ἱμάτιον: n.n., garment, clothes
ἵνα: conj., in order that, (adv.,
where)
ἴσος: adj., equal to
ἰσχύω: v., be strong, have force
ἴσως: adv., perhaps, equally

K
καθάπτω: v., tie on, fasten, (mid.)
upbraid, assail
καθεύδω: v., sleep
καθομολογέω: v., confess
καιρός: n.m., right time,
opportunity
κακία: n.f., wickedness
κακός: adj., bad, wicked
κακουργέω: v., do evil to
καλέω: v., call, summon
καλλωπίζω: v., beautify
καλός: adj., fine, noble, excellent
καλῶς: adv., well, excellently
κατά: prep., (+gen.) against,
(+acc.) according to, down
καταγέλαστος: adj., ridiculous

κατάγελως: n.m., ridicule,
absurdity, laughing-stock
κατάδηλος: adj., very plain, clear
καταλείπω: leave behind,
abandon
καταφρονέω: v., despise, look
down on
κελεύω: v., order, request, bid
κήδομαι: v., be concerned for
κινδυνεύω: v., run a risk, be in
danger, be likely
κίνδυνος: n.m., danger
κοινῇ: adv., in common
κοινός: adj., common, public
κοινωνέω: v., partake in, have a
share of
κομίζω: v., supply, provide for
κορυβαντιάω: v., celebrate the
Korybantic rites
κόσμιος: adj., well-ordered,
regular
Κρήτη: n.f., Crete
κρίνω: v., judge, decide
κύριος: adj., having authority,
n.m., lord, master

Λ
λαμβάνω: v., take, receive, catch
λανθάνω: v., escape notice
λέγω: v., say, speak, tell, mean
λευκός: adj., white, bright
λίαν: adv., too much
λογίζομαι: v., consider, reckon,
calculate
λόγος: n.m., word, speech,
reasoning
λοιπός: adj., remaining
λυπέω: v., grieve, give pain to
λύπη: n.f., grief, pain
λωβάομαι: v., maim, maltreat

M

μά: *partic. of exclamation*, μὰ τὸν Δία, by Zeus!

μακάριος: *adj.*, blessed, happy

μάλα: *adv.*, very, very much

μάλιστα: *adv.*, especially, most of all

μᾶλλον: *adv.*, rather

μάτην: *adv.*, in vain

μέγας: *adj.*, great, much

μέλλω: *v.*, be about to, intend

μέλω: *v.*, be an object of care, μέλει μοι(*impers.*) it is a care (to me, etc.)

μέμφομαι: *v.*, blame

μέντοι: *conj.*, however, but

μένω: *v.*, remain, stay, abide by (an opinion)

μέρος: *n.n.*, part, portion, share

μετά: *prep.*, (+*gen.*) with, (+*acc.*), after

μεταδίδωμι: *v.*, give a share of

μεταλλάσσω: *v.*, exchange, alter

μετοικέω: *v.*, migrate

μετρίως: *adv.*, moderately

μηδαμῶς: *adv.*, by no means

μήπω: *adv.*, not yet

μήτε...μήτε: *conj.*, neither...nor

μήτηρ: *n.f.*, mother

μικρός: *adj.*, small, little

μοῖρα: *n.f.*, portion, lot, due reverence

μόνος: *adj.*, only, alone

μορμολύττομαι: *v.*, frighten, scare

μουσικός: *adj.*, musical, μουσική (τέχνη): the musical art

μοχθηρός: *adj.*, wretched, sorely distressed

N

ναί: *adv.*, *used for strong affirmation*, yes, certainly

νέος: *adj.*, new, young

νή: *partic.*, by (in oaths)

νόμιμος: *adj.*, lawful, customary; τὰ νόμιμα: *n.pl.*, usages, customs

νόμος: *n.m.*, law, custom

νοσώδης: *adj.*, sickly, ailing

νοῦς: *n.m.*, mind, thought, reason

νῦν, νυνί: *adv.*, now

νύξ: *n.f.*, night

Ξ

ξένος: *n.m.*, stranger, guest, friend

ξυγχωρέω: *v.*, concede, yield

ξύμπας: *adj.*, all together, the whole

ξυμφορά: *n.f.*, event, chance

ξυνδιαταλαιπωρέω: *v.*, to endure hardship with

ξυνδοκέω: *v.*, seem good (to several), ξυνδοκεῖ: *impers.*, it is agreed

ξύνειμι: *v.*, be with

ξυνήθης: *adj.*, accustomed, usual, intimate with

ξυνθήκη: *n.f.*, agreement, covenant

ξυντίθημι: *v.*, put together, (*mid.*) agree on

O

ὅδε: *dem. pron.*, this (man, etc.)

οἶδα: *v.*, know

οἴομαι: *v.*, think, suppose

οἷος: *rel. pron.*, of what sort. οἷός τε: able

οἴχομαι: *v.*, be gone, depart

ὀλίγος: *adj.*, small, little

ὅμοιος: *adj.*, like

ὁμολογέω: *v.*, agree to, acknowledge, confess

ὁμολογία: *n.f.*, agreement, assent

ὅμως: *adv.*, nevertheless, still

ὀνίνημι: v., profit, benefit
ὀνομάζω: v., name, speak of, call
ὅποι: adv., whither
ὅπως: adv., how, in what way, in order that
ὁράω: v., see
ὀρθότης: n.f., straightness, rightness
ὄρθρος: n.m., pre-dawn twighlight
ὀρθός: adj., right, straight
ὀρφανία: n.f., orphaned state
ὀρφανός: adj., orphaned
ὅς: rel. pron., who
ὅσιος: adj., pious, holy, devout
ὅσος: rel. pron., as much as, as great as
ὅσπερ: rel. pron., the very man who
ὅστις: indef. pron., whoever
ὁστισοῦν: indef. pron., anyone whatever
ὅτε: conj., when
ὅτι: conj., that, because
οὐδαμόσε: adv., to no place
οὐδαμῶς: adv., in no way, by no means
οὐδέ: conj., nor, not even
οὐδείς: num. adj., no one
οὐδέτερος: adj., neither
οὐκέτι: adv., no more, no longer
οὐκοῦν: adv., surely (in questions inviting assent)
οὔκουν: partic., certainly not, (in questions), and so not?
οὖν: partic., so, therefore, then
οὐσία: n.f., property
οὗτος: dem. pron., this man etc.
οὕτω: adv., so, thus
ὀφείλω: v., owe; εἰ γάρ ὤφελον: would that
ὄφελος: n.n., advantage, profit, aid

Π
παιδεία: n.f., education
παιδεύω: v., teach, educate
παιδιά: n.f., child's play, amusement
παιδοτρίβης: n.m., physical trainer
παῖς: n.m. or f., child
πάλαι: adv., long ago, in the old days
πανταχοῦ: adv., everywhere
πάνυ: adv., entirely, completely
παρά: prep., (+gen.) from, by, (+dat.) by, at, (+acc.) along, to the side of, towards, against
παραβαίνω: v., go beyond, transgress
παραγγέλλω: v., exhort, recommend, order
παρακάθημαι: v., sit beside, sit near
παρακρούω: v., lead astray, deceive
παραμένω: v., stand beside, stand fast
πάρειμι: v., be present
παρέχω: v., supply, provide, cause
παρίστημι: v., set, place near
πᾶς: adj., all, every
πάσχω: v., suffer
πατήρ: n.m., father
πατρίς: n.f., native land
παύω: v., make to stop, (mid.) cease
πείθω: v., persuade, (mid.) obey, trust
πειράομαι: v., attempt, try, have experience of
περί: prep., (+gen.) about, round, concerning, (+dat.) in regard to, (+acc.) about, in the case of.
περιμένω: v., wait, await, delay

104

περιτίθημι: *v.*, place around, (*mid.*) put on
πῃ: *partic.*, in some way
πηνίκα: *adv.* at what point of time?
πλεῖστος: *adj.*, (*superl.* πολύς), most, greatest
πλείων: *adj.*, (*comp.* πολύς), more
πλημμελής: *adj.*, out of tune, out of keeping
πλησιάζω: *v.*, associate with, bring near
πλοῖον: *n.n.*, ship
πόθεν: *adv.*, whence?
ποῖ: *adv.*, where to?
ποι: *adv.*, to somewhere
ποιέω: *v.*, make, do, act, compose
πολέμιος: *adj.*, hostile, warlike
πόλεμος: *n.m.*, battle, war
πόλις: *n.f.*, city
πολιτεία: *n.f.*, state, government, administration
πολιτεύομαι: *v.*, function as a citizen
πολίτης: *n.m.*, citizen
πολλάκις: *adv.*, often
πολλαχοῦ: *adv.*, in many places
πολύς: *adj.*, much
πονηρός: *adj.*, bad, worthless
ποτε: *adv.*, at some time, ever
ποτέον: *verbal adj.*, (from πίνω) one must drink
πότερον: *adv.*, whether
που: *adv.*, somewhere, (I suppose)
ποῦ: *adv.*, where?
πρᾶγμα: *n.n.*, affair, work, trouble
πρᾶξις: *n.f.*, action, affair, matter
πρᾶος: *adj.*, mild, gentle
πράττω: *v.*, do, make, practise
πρεσβεύω: *v.*, pay respect to, revere, esteem

πρίν: *adv.*, before
πρό: *prep.*, before, rather than
προαγορεύω: *v.*, proclaim
προαιρέω: *v.*, choose, prefer
πρόγονος: *n.m.*, ancestor
προδίδωμι: *v.*, betray, abandon
προθυμέομαι: *v.*, desire eagerly, strive
προθυμία: *n.f.*, good will, concern
προμηθέομαι: *v.*, take thought beforehand
πρός: *prep.*, (+acc.) to, towards, against (+gen.) in the presence of, in the name of, (+dat.) in addition to
προσέρχομαι: *v.*, approach, visit
προσέχω: *v.*, apply, turn (attention) towards
πρόσθεν: *adv.*, before, formerly
προστάττω: *v.*, command, order
πρόσωπον: *n.n.*, face, person
πρότερον: *adv.*, sooner, before
προτίθημι: *v.*, set before, propose
πρῴ: *adv.*, early in the day
πρῶτος: *adj.*, first
πώποτε: *adv.*, ever yet
πῶς: *adv.*, how?
πως: *adv.*, somehow, in some way

P
ῥάδιος: *adj.*, easy
ῥάθυμος: *adj.*, easy-tempered, careless, easy
ῥήτωρ: *n.m.*, orator, public speaker

Σ
σαυτόν: *reflex. pron.*, yourself
σαφῶς: *adv.*, clearly
σέβομαι: *v.*, worship, pay regard to
σεμνός: *adj.*, solemn, holy
σιγή: *n.f.*, silence

σκέμμα: *n.n.*, speculation
σκέπτομαι: *v.*, consider, examine
σκευή: *n.f.*, dress, attire
σκέψις: *n.f.*, consideration, reflexion
σκοπέω: *v.*, consider, examine, contemplate
σμικρός: *adj.*, little, small
σός: *possess. adj.*, your
σοφός: *adj.*, wise,
σπεύδω: *v.*, urge on, seek eagerly, hasten
σπουδή: *n.f.*, haste, earnestness, trouble
στερέω: *v.*, deprive, bereave
στρατεύω: *v.*, serve as a soldier
συκοφάντης: *n.m.*, informer
συχνός: *adj.*, frequent, much, long (of time)
σφόδρα: *adv.*, exceedingly, earnestly
σχεδόν: *adv.*, almost, nearly
σχῆμα: *n.n.*, appearance
σῴζω: *v.*, save
σῶμα: *n.n.*, body

T
τάξις: *n.f.*, arrangement, drawing up
τάττω: *v.*, arrange, put in order
τείνω: *v.*, extend, stretch
τεκμαίρομαι: *v.*, judge, decree, estimate
τεκμήριον: *n.n.*, proof, sure sign
τελευταῖος: *adj.*, last
τελευτάω: *v.*, accomplish, die
τελέω: *v.*, fulfil, pay as due
τηλικόσδε: *adj.*, of such an age
τηλικοῦτος: *adj.*, see τηλικόσδε
τήμερον: *adv.*, today
τηνικάδε: *adv.*, at this time of day, so early

τιμάω: *v.*, honour, revere, (*mid.*) estimate a penalty
τιμή: *n.f.*, honour, esteem
τίμιος: *adj.*, valued, esteemed
τιτρώσκω: *v.*, wound, hurt
τίς: *interrog. pron.*, who?
τις: *indef. pron.*, someone, a certain one
τοι: *partic.*, in truth, actually
τοίνυν: *partic.*, so then, therefore
τοιοῦτος: *dem. adj.*, of this kind, such
τολμάω: *v.*, dare, venture
τόπος: *n.m.*, place
τοσοῦτος: *dem. adj.*, so great, so much
τότε: *adv.*, then
τουτί: for τοῦτο (see οὗτος)
τρέφω: *v.*, nourish, bring up
τρίτατος: *adj.*, third
τριχῆ: *adv.*, in three ways
τρόπος: *n.m.*, manner, way
τροφεύς: *n.m.*, foster-father
τροφή: *n.f.*, food, nurture, rearing
τυγχάνω: *v.*, happen, (*with pres. part.* εἰμί) (happen to) be
τύπτω: *v.*, strike, beat
τυφλός: *adj.*, blind
τυχή: *n.f.*, chance, accident

Y
ὑγιεινός: *adj.*, healthy, sound
υἱός: *n.m.*, son
ὑπακούω: *v.*, heed, regard
ὑπάρχω: *v.*, begin, be sufficient, (ὑπάρχει + *dat.*) it is possible (for me etc.)
ὑπείκω: *v.*, retire, yield
ὑπέρ: *prep.*, (+*acc.*) beyond, (+*gen.*) on behalf of, over
ὑπέρχομαι: *v.*, come under, insinuate into another's good graces

ὑπό: *prep.*, (+*acc.*) under, (+*gen.*)
 by, (+*dat.*) under
ὑποβλέπω: *v.*, look askance at
ὑποδέχομαι: *v.*, welcome,
 entertain
ὑπολογίζομαι: *v.*, take into
 consideration
ὑστεραῖος: *adj.*, the following
 (day)
ὑφηγέομαι: *v.*, guide, direct

Φ
φαίνω: *v.*, show, shine, (*mid.*)
 appear
φάσκω: *v.*, say, assert
φαῦλος: *adj.*, worthless, mean
φέρω: *v.*, bear, bring
φεύγω: *v.*, flee from, escape
φημί: *v.*, say, speak, mean
φίλος: *adj.*, friendly, dear, (*n.m.*)
 a friend
φλυαρία: *n.f.*, nonsense
φοβέω: *v.*, frighten, (*mid.*) fear
φοιτάω: *v.*, visit, frequent
φράζω: *v.*, declare, tell, explain
φρόνιμος: *adj.*, sensible, prudent
φροντίζω: *v.*, think of, consider,
 reflect
φυγή: *n.f.*, flight, exile
φύλαξ: *n.m.*, guard
φυτεύω: *v.*, beget, produce
φύω: *v.*, grow, produce, put forth,
 be born, (πεφυκώς, (*perf*). by
 nature)

Χ
χαίρω: *v.*, rejoice (ἐὰν χαίρειν:
 put from one's mind)
χαλεπαίνω: *v.*, be angry with
χαλεπός: *adj.*, difficult, hard
χάρις: *n.f.*, gratitude, favour,
 thanks
χράομαι: *v.*, use, experience

χρή: *v. impers.*, it is necessary,
 one ought
χρῆμα: *n.n.*, thing, matter, (*pl.*)
 money
χρηστός: *adj.*, good, true,
 beneficial, serviceable
χρόνος: *n.m.*, time
χωλός: *adj.*, lame
χωρίς: *adv. and prep.*, (+*gen.*)
 apart, without

Ψ
ψόγος: *n.m.*, blame, censure

Ω
ὦ: *mode of address* (eg. ὦ
 Σώκρατες)
ᾧδε: *adv.*, thus, in this way
ὥρα: *n.f.*, hour, time
ὡς: *adv.*, how, as, (*conj.*) when,
 since, in order that,
 (*prep.*+*acc.*) towards
ὥσπερ: *conj.*, just as, (*adv.*) as it
 were
ὥστε: *conj.*, so that

CPSIA information can be obtained at www.ICGtesting.com
Printed in the USA
LVOW12s2235240714

395965LV00013B/226/P